France History

The Fascinating History of Ancient and Modern France

(An Enthralling Guide to a Major Event in World History)

James Miller

Published By **Andrew Zen**

James Miller

All Rights Reserved

France History: The Fascinating History of Ancient and Modern France (An Enthralling Guide to a Major Event in World History)

ISBN 978-1-7771142-4-4

No part of this guidebook shall be reproduced in any form without permission in writing from the publisher except in the case of brief quotations embodied in critical articles or reviews.

Legal & Disclaimer

The information contained in this book is not designed to replace or take the place of any form of medicine or professional medical advice. The information in this book has been provided for educational & entertainment purposes only.

The information contained in this book has been compiled from sources deemed reliable, and it is accurate to the best of the Author's knowledge; however, the Author cannot guarantee its accuracy and validity and cannot be held liable for any errors or omissions. Changes are periodically made to this book. You must consult your doctor or get professional medical advice before using any of the suggested remedies, techniques, or information in this book.

Upon using the information contained in this book, you agree to hold harmless the Author from and against any damages, costs, and expenses, including any legal fees potentially resulting from the application of any of the information provided by this guide. This disclaimer applies to any damages or injury caused by the use and application, whether directly or indirectly, of any advice or information presented, whether for breach of contract, tort, negligence, personal injury, criminal intent, or under any other cause of action.

You agree to accept all risks of using the information presented inside this book. You need to consult a professional medical practitioner in order to ensure you are both able and healthy enough to participate in this program.

Table Of Contents

Chapter 1: Prehistoric And Ancient France 1

Chapter 2: France In The Middle Ages 8

Chapter 3: France Within The 16th Century 20

Chapter 4: The Prelude To The French Revolution 29

Chapter 5: The Great Fear And The Abolition Of Feudalism.......................... 36

Chapter 6: France Inside The 19th Century 51

Chapter 7: Contemporary France........... 72

Chapter 8: The Government Underneath Hollande 80

Chapter 9: The Macron Presidency 93

Chapter 10: The Top 10 Reasons To Visit France... 99

Chapter 11: Tourist Attractions In France 119

Chapter 12: Ideal France Five-Days Itineraries 130

Chapter 13: Obtaining France Tourist Visa 142

Chapter 14: France Travel Cost 152

Chapter 15: France Cultural Custom 169

Chapter 16: Boeuf Bourguignon........... 178

Chapter 1: Prehistoric And Ancient France

In the annals of statistics, you'll be capable of trace the footsteps of the Cro-Magnon human beings, who continued through the icy, encompass of the final bloodless duration in France. These were hardy cave dwellers, their survival hinging upon the pork of mammoths and reindeer. Resilient and revolutionary, they have to were, to bear such unforgiving situations. The Cro-Magnons etched their name within the annals of time, famed for the paintings of artwork adorning cave partitions and the elaborate figures normal from ivory.

The era of hunter-gatherer manner of existence slowly waned, fading into obscurity with the taking flight ice age. Although farming's origins lay within the cradle of the Middle East, France took its first tentative steps into the location of agriculture round 6,000 BC. The transition from a existence of foraging and looking to the toil of farming grow to be an difficult journey, an evolution spanning endless generations Hunting, notwithstanding the fact that clung to its role as a critical source of sustenance.

Around 4,500 BC, the Stone Age farmers had ushered in a complicated civilization. Their hands molded menhirs, the ones stoic reputation stones, and the grandeur of massive stone graves. In the embryonic levels, French farmers wielded stone system, but round 2,000 BC, the alchemy of metal entered their lives. By 900 B.C., a fixed that might later undergo the names Celts and Gauls descended upon France, armed with iron implements and weapons.

Within the ranks of the Celts, a social hierarchy emerged, with the aristocracy reigning ideal. Below them toiled the farmers and artisans, their recognition much less extended. It become the Celtic artisans who excelled in the craft of working with metals, forging iron, copper, and casting gold into wondrous paperwork.

Hill forts rose, castles of their time, shaping the inspiration of what could evolve into current-day French towns. Commerce flowed thru those budding facilities, respiration existence into the area. Then, in 600 BC, the Greeks, driven with the resource of manner of ambition and exchange, planted the seeds of Marseilles. These interactions strong vital change links among the Mediterranean and Gaul.

Yet, the Gauls, but their wealthy ancient past, had been plagued thru inner divisions. Over 60 tribes stood as the constructing blocks of their society, in the end proving their Achilles' heel. The Romans, prepared and bold, located an opportunity in this fragmentation.

Roman France

In 121 BC, the Romans started out their conquest of a southern fragment of France, christened due to the fact the province in the language of Latin - a province appeared to modernity as Provence. However, it modified into in fifty eight BC, the dawn of a modern day technology, that Julius Caesar unfurled the banner of Roman dominion, embarking on a advertising marketing campaign to carry the whole lot of Gaul beneath his rule.

It was not till 52 BC that a valiant chieftain named Vercingetorix rallied the Gauls in competition to the Roman juggernaut. Yet, the fortunes of war desired Caesar, culminating inside the pivotal Battle of Alesia. The Gauls, their spirit unyielding but their forces depleted, had little recourse but to submit to the yoke of Roman manipulate.

Henceforth, the Romans undertook the grand mission of building a web of roadways crisscrossing Gaul. These thoroughfares enabled their legions to march swiftly and decisively from one prevent of the land to the alternative. By 40 three BC, the venerable Lugdunum, that may metamorphose into Lyon, turned into anointed because the capital of Gaul, and the empire sowed the seeds of numerous new towns beneath the benevolent reign of Emperor Augustus.

Slowly but genuinely, the Gauls embraced, at the least in component, Roman lifestyle. Latin have become their lingua franca, and some of the Gallic populace end up bestowed with the coveted mantle of Roman citizenship, reaping its manifold privileges. After the three hundred and sixty five days 48 AD, a cadre of Gauls ascended to the lofty ranks of Roman senators, having proved their mettle in administrative roles inner Gaul.

Even because the first century unfurled, Christianity located its way into the coronary coronary coronary heart of France. Yet, the course for early Christians turn out to be fraught with peril, as persecutions weighed heavy upon them. In the twelve months 250 AD, a person known as Denis met a ugly surrender, his life snuffed out thru the executioner's blade. Time would render him France's client saint.

Nevertheless, the Roman Empire, a behemoth of antiquity, started to remedy inside the mid-1/3 century. Inflation spiraled out of manage, and plagues solid their darkish shadow internationally. Rome, decided for assets, imposed heavy levies, the usage of some peasants from their fields to are attempting to find refuge a number of the outlaws.

Meanwhile, the Germanic peoples, warriors of the north, marauded sooner or later of France in the route of the 0.33 century. The Roman Emperor Diocletian, in some unspecified time in the future of his rule from 284 to 305, initiated sweeping reforms in Gaul's governance in a bid to stave off coming near near crumble. This intervention prolonged the life of Roman France for a few different century.

Yet, the fates had charted a distinct route. In December of the one year 406 AD, a coalition of Germanic tribes surged into Gaul. Even the robust Romans found themselves powerless to stem the tide. At first, the ones Germanic novices paid reluctant obeisance to Roman authority. But with the Empire's final gasp, they set up their very personal dominions upon the soil of France.

By the year 500 AD, the Franks, destined to lend their name to the land, claimed dominion over northern France. Clovis, a call etched into the annals of Frankish data from 481 to 511, stood at their helm. He orchestrated a momentous shift in religion, steering the Franks within the path of Christianity. With a shared perception, the animosity many of the Franks and the Romano-Gallic population started out out to wither away, their cultures entwining as they intermarried.

In the tapestry of France's history, the threads of time weave a complex and numerous story, one which transcends epochs, empires, and cultures. As the centuries rolled on, France must maintain to adapt, taking over new shapes and identities, but typically keeping the echoes of its storied past.

Chapter 2: France In The Middle Ages

It modified into inside the three hundred and sixty five days 507 A.D. That Clovis, a effective chief of the Franks, said the quaint metropolis of Paris as his capital. A massive turning element within the annals of history, this announcement became determined with the resource of the ebook of a hard and rapid of guidelines called Salic regulation. The fall of Roman power inside the fifth century had strong a pall over the as quickly as-thriving French cities, regardless of the reality that they controlled to go through.

Clovis, a conqueror of great ambition, extended his dominion even to the southern reaches of France. His successors carried the torch of his legacy following his lack of lifestyles in 511, at the mild age of forty five. By the center of the 6th century, the Franks, under their leadership, reigned final over all of France.

However, the grip of the Merovingians, the first dynasty of Frankish rulers, remained tenuous at notable in France's peripheral regions. Provence and Burgundy retained vestiges of autonomy, as did Brittany, a region that had witnessed an inflow of humans from southern England in the path of the fifth century.

As the tapestry of time unfold out, the seventh century observed a sluggish erosion of authority for the Merovingian rulers. While they held symbolic importance, they garnered a popularity as useless leaders. This decline paved the way for the ascendancy of the Carolingians, a family marked with the aid of huge estates and wealth. Their hereditary position as "mayor of the palace" conferred upon them a completely particular position of electricity.

In the three hundred and sixty five days 751, Pepin the Short, the inaugural ruler of the Carolingian dynasty, deposed the very last vestiges of Merovingian royalty, marking a decisive shift within the annals of French information. His son, Charles Martel, etched his name in records with the beneficial useful resource of triumphing over the Islamic forces within the pivotal Battle of Poitiers in 732. Victorious against the Bavarians and Saxons, Charles Martel's legacy endured through his son, Charlemagne.

The latter continued his father's artwork and oversaw the status quo of a exquisite empire that stretched at some point of the European expanse. With a combination of international family members and coercion, Charlemagne "converted" non-Christian Germans and, in the 12 months 800 AD, became anointed Emperor via the Pope. Thus, Charlemagne forged himself because the present day Roman Emperor.

To consistent the church's assist, Charlemagne launched right into a grand agency, building numerous monasteries and donating giant tracts of territory to spiritual establishments. His reign moreover witnessed a cultural renaissance, a length now referred to as the Carolingian Renaissance.

The mantle of strength eventually passed from Charlemagne within the 12 months 814, and his successor, Louis the Pious, decreed that the empire could be divided among his sons upon his eventual passing. In 840, Louis breathed his final, and the Treaty of Verdun in 843 sealed the fate of the Frankish realm. It come to be severed in two, with Charles the Bald presiding over the western half of from 838 to 877. As time wove its complex tapestry, the nascent country of France started out out to take shape.

Towards the stop of the 8th century, France faced peril from Arab incursions originating in North Africa. Yet, more menacing but were the Viking raids that marauded through the 9th and 10th centuries. The French monarchs, outmatched thru the relentless invaders, sooner or later ceded authority to shut by means of magnates who undertook the obligation of protecting their beleaguered subjects. The South observed the emergence of more and more self enough regions, at the equal time as Brittany held rapid to its independence inside the northwest.

The turning component got here in 911 while Charles the Simple and Rollo, the formidable Viking leader, placed aside their versions and inked a peace %. In go back for embracing Christianity and swearing allegiance to Charles, Rollo become granted the land now known as Normandy.

With the Viking threat abated, Hugh Capet ascended to the throne in 987, marking the set up order of the Capetian dynasty. However, the French monarchs had relinquished plenty of their former authority with the resource of this juncture, with counts and dukes exercise first-rate autonomy. The region underneath Capetian manage emerge as restricted, spanning a tiny territory within the vicinity of Paris.

Events took a greater complex flip at the same time as, in 1066, William, Duke of Normandy, seized the English crown, growing a dual characteristic in the French monarchy.

As King of England, he stood on an equal footing with the King of France. The complexities extended further at the equal time as, within the mid-12th century, Henry, Count of Anjou, wedded Eleanor of Aquitaine and come to be topped King of England in 1154. From that component onward, English monarchs wielded authority over a splendid portion of France.

However, in 1202, King Philip II of France waged struggle in opposition to King John of England and triumphed, claiming the lion's proportion of John's territory in France. Philip's reign found a full-size growth of the French monarchy's territory. His grandson, Louis IX (1226-1270), persevered this style, and through the late thirteenth century, the rulers of France held sway over the whole thing of the land. Yet, wallet of autonomy continued, with Aquitaine under English rule, at the same time as Brittany and Burgundy retained severa stages of independence.

The Valois Rule France

As the annals of statistics unfurled, the reign of King Philip the Fair of France, spanning from 1285 to 1314, marked a normal eastward expansion of his realm, finished via strategic marriages and astute acquisitions. France's monetary machine flourished in tandem with the ones territorial profits. Thriving cities bore witness to the burgeoning exchange that enriched the kingdom, with Paris, via the use of the 11th century, growing as a thriving metropolis.

The flourishing of the arts left an indelible mark on the French landscape, encompassing a rich tapestry of architectural marvels, sculpted masterpieces, and the written word. The 12th century heralded the start of Paris University, located via the use of the repute quo of Toulouse University in 1229, Montpellier University in 1289, Avignon University in 1304 and 1306, and Angers University in 1337.

Meanwhile, the epoch of the Valois dynasty dawned with the passing of Charles the Fair, the closing monarch of the Capetians, in 1328. Philip of Valois, Charles's cousin, ascended the throne as Philip VI. However, a shadow of battle loomed, for King Charles the Fair's sister come to be the mom of Edward III of England, a claimant to the French crown. Salic regulation barred Edward from inheriting the throne through a girl relative. The flames of an extended and bloody struggle ignited between England and France, and this conflagration ought to persist till 1337.

In the one year 1340, the English military completed a powerful victory over the French at Sluys, and the longbow emerged as a sport-changer within the pivotal 1346 Battle of Crecy, fundamental to an English triumph. The harrowing specter of the Black Death returned in 1348, reaping a grim harvest of almost a 3rd of the populace in each England and France.

Notwithstanding the scourge of the plague, the English secured a decisive victory inside the Battle of Poitiers in 1356, and years later, they captured the French king, John II. The English demanded a full-size ransom for John, main to unrest some of the beleaguered population. In 1358, this discontent boiled over into a huge rebellion known as the Jacquerie, unexpectedly quelled thru the government.

France's fortunes took a sour turn with the signing of the Treaty of Bretigny in 1360, which charge the u . S . A . Sizeable territorial losses. The short interlude of peace become shattered in 1369 as hostilities resumed. By 1375, the French forces had reversed their fortunes, forcing the English to retreat to a handful of coastal ports.

The 3 hundred and sixty 5 days 1392 introduced a shadow over France, as King Charles VI descended into madness. An excessive power war erupted, with severa factions vying for manipulate of the kingdom. The Duke of Burgundy, Jean sans Peur (John the Fearless), led one faction, at the same time as the opposing organisation rallied at the back of the king's brother, the Duke of Orleans. Tragedy marred this political strife whilst the Duke of Orleans became assassinated, and in 1415, the English invaded all over again, accomplishing a splendid victory at Agincourt.

By 1419, the Duke of Burgundy met a similar destiny, however the Burgundians later long-established an alliance with the English. Henry V of England became officially identified because of the reality the rightful king of France, and that they coerced Charles VI into betrothing his daughter to Henry. The Dauphin, Charles's son, sought secure haven inside the south, leaving the English and Burgundians on top of things of northern France.

In 1429, a notable turning factor emerged with the arrival of Jeanne d'Arc (Joan of Arc), whose impact ignited a country wide renaissance in France. Joan's tale modified into a unusual one, marked via the usage of the claim that she received divine "voices" and her penchant for sporting guys's apparel. At the gentle age of 13, she began to pay attention those "voices," their origins shrouded in thriller. In an era bereft of advanced scientific knowledge, her circumstance might be seemed pretty in any other case in recent times, with capability remedies and assist.

Nonetheless, Joan of Arc succeeded in persuading the French king to entrust her with the manage of the army inside the pivotal Battle of Orleans in 1429. Prior to her intervention, the English had besieged the city, however at the side of her steerage, they were compelled to retreat. Tragically, in 1430, Joan became captured through the Burgundians, who in the end passed her over to the English. In 1431, she became tried for heresy and burned at the stake.

However, the French counteroffensive continued unabated. By 1453, the English had been expelled from France, with Calais reputation as the only exception.

The overcome the English allowed the French monarchs to reclaim Aquitaine, Normandy, and Burgundy. Their dominion prolonged to first-rate corners of France, with Provence turning into part of the place in 1482. The independence of Brittany become curtailed whilst Charles VIII, who reigned from 1483 to 1498, wed Anne, Duchess of Brittany, in 1491. As the fifteenth century drew to a near, France had coalesced proper into a unified and strong monarchy.

Chapter 3: France Within The 16th Century

The early 16th century heralded a length of sturdy monetary boom and populace enlargement in France. In 1539, the decree of Villers-Cotterets marked a massive milestone with the resource of converting Latin with French due to the truth the language for all legitimate files. Nevertheless, many individuals decided on to keep speaking Breton and Occitan an in preference to embracing the emerging French.

Amid this period of transformation, France engaged in an extended collection of conflicts with Italy, spanning from 1494 to 1559, most effective finding respite with the Treaty of Cateau-Cambresis.

Simultaneously, the Reformation solid its turbulent shadow over France In 1523, Jean Valliere, a French Protestant, have become the u . S . A .'s first martyr. Persecution of Protestants escalated after 1540, coinciding with the upward thrust of a present day strand of Protestantism referred to as Calvinism in 1541.

Tensions among Catholics and Protestants erupted into violence even as Catholics killed numerous Protestants in Vassy in 1562. The years 1562–1563, 1567–1568, 1569–1570, 1573–1574, 1576–1577, 1579–1580, and 1585–1598 witnessed a succession of spiritual conflicts that marred the state.

The darkest bankruptcy of these conflicts opened up at some stage in the St. Bartholomew's Day Massacre, in which up to three,000 Protestants fell victim to the violence perpetrated by means of the usage of Catholics in Paris. Similar atrocities carried out out in distinctive French cities, claiming an predicted eight,000 greater Protestant lives.

The assassination of King Henry III in 1589 created a contentious scenario, with the Protestant Henry of Navarre growing due to the reality the heir obvious to the French throne. Many Catholics destructive Henry's claim, forcing him to wage a regular battle for his rule. Ultimately, in 1593, he converted to Catholicism, and the subsequent 365 days, he made his effective access into Paris. It come to be below his reign that the Edict of Nantes modified into in the end promulgated in 1598, granting Protestants the right to preserve fortified cities and exercising their religion without fear of persecution.

Yet, the demanding situations confronted by way of way of using France towards the end of the 16th century were no longer confined to spiritual strife. The country weathered a sequence of poor harvests and devastating epidemics in the course of the 1580s and 1590s, confronting a harsh and checking out period in its history.

France in the 17th Century

The 17th century marked an technology of constant consolidation of royal authority in France, culminating within the repute quo of an absolute monarchy by the use of the century's close to. The announcement of Louis XIV, "L'etat c'est moi" (I am the dominion), encapsulated the absolutist ideology that reigned exceptional.

Yet, future took an unforeseen turn in France, at the same time as Catholic extremist Francois Ravaillac assassinated King Henry IV in 1610, thrusting Louis XIII onto the throne inside the equal 365 days. Cardinal Richelieu, who assumed the mantle of leader minister in 1624 and retained strength till his dying in 1642, exerted a profound affect over the monarch all through most of his reign.

During the early 17th century, Huguenots, the French Protestants, sought to installation solid enclaves. Louis XIII, however, remained steadfast in his aim of assimilating them into the nation. The metropolis of La Rochelle have end up a focal point of this ambition, primary to a royal siege in 1627, quelled pleasant after a brutal and continual standoff that lasted until 1628.

In the broader European context, the Thirty Years War ignited in 1618, drawing in more than one European powers, along side Austria and Spain. In 1635, Cardinal Richelieu entered the fray at the aspect of the anti-Habsburg coalition, fearing that the encirclement of France could give up end result from Habsburg dominance.

Ultimately, France emerged effective from the struggle, with the 12 months 1643 witnessing French forces making wonderful inroads at the japanese the front after their decisive victory over the Spanish at Rocroi.

However, the value of the warfare necessitated extensive tax will boom, triggering a series of revolts during France. Western revolts erupted in 1636, located by way of a Normandy rebellion in 1639, each rapidly quelled through manner of way of the authorities. The struggle with Spain persevered till 1659 however concluded with Austria in 1648.

In the midst of those stressful conditions, Louis XIV ascended to the French throne in 1643, incomes the moniker "the Sun King" and destined to emerge as one of the united states of america's most illustrious monarchs.

Early in his reign, France faced upheaval in the form of the Fronde, a sequence of uprisings that transpired among 1648 and 1652. Noble factions, keen to guard their feudal privileges in competition to the growing authority of the monarchy, organized those revolts. The government, but, suppressed the Fronde, leaving Louis XIV more potent than ever in its aftermath.

In 1661, Louis XIV made a pivotal choice, opting to dispense with the offerings of a top minister. He relied on the capable financial minister Colbert until 1683, steering the course of the u . S . With an unwavering hand.

The Age of Louis XIV

Louis XIV's reign marked the zenith of French art work and era. In 1661, the Academy of Dance changed into established, paving the way for an era of resourceful and intellectual flourishing. The following years witnessed the formation of the Science Academy in 1666, the Architecture Academy in 1671, and the Music Academy in 1672. By 1682, Louis XIV had moved his court docket docket to the newly built and similarly grand Palace of Versailles.

However, amidst those cultural and medical improvements, Louis XIV embroiled France in a series of fundamental wars that spanned from 1667 to 1713. The War of Devolution (1667–1668), the War of Dutch Succession (1672–1678), the War of the League of Augsburg (1689–1697), and the War of Spanish Succession (1701–1713) left a significant toll at the state. To finance those steeply-priced conflicts, taxes have been substantially raised, burdening the common citizens.

In addition to the strains of war, non secular freedom for Protestants suffered a grave setback even as Louis revoked the Edict of Nantes in 1685. This brought approximately the exodus of masses of heaps of France's brightest minds as Protestants sought shelter from persecution. The duration turn out to be further marred with the aid of the use of devastating famines in 1693–1694 and 1707–1710, marking the maximum extreme in France's information.

Eighteenth-Century France

The 18th century saw financial prosperity for lots French residents, despite the fact that severe poverty remained a chronic challenge, because it did in most nations in the course of this era. Business and change improved unexpectedly, and the population of France professional first rate growth, with a burgeoning center elegance growing some of the wealthy and the impoverished.

This century additionally witnessed the Age of Enlightenment, characterised via the ascendancy of rationalist philosophers like Voltaire (1694–1778) and Denis Diderot (1713–1784). These intellectuals at a loss for words the have an effect on of the Catholic church and traditional jail and political structures, at the same time as courses critiquing the prevailing order proliferated.

Many nicely-knowledgeable French citizens appeared to Britain as a model to emulate, inspired via England's parliamentary governance, spiritual tolerance, and protections in opposition to arbitrary imprisonment. Voltaire, specifically, praised England in his writings after travelling in 1726.

However, France became embroiled in the Seven Years' War (1756–1763), resulting in the loss of the French Empire's territories in Canada and India.

In 1776, the North American colonies of Britain declared independence, with France presenting crucial useful resource to the American revolutionaries of their quest for liberty. France formally entered the conflict in 1778, which done a pivotal function within the United States' remaining victory at Yorktown in 1781. In 1783, Britain cited the independence of the American colonies underneath strain.

Chapter 4: The Prelude To The French Revolution

The seeds of the French Revolution were sown amidst developing unrest most of the the Aristocracy. While theoretically, the king possessed absolute authority, it have emerge as obtrusive that his strength had barriers after 1774. Groups known as "parlements," crafted from aristocrats, performed a pivotal characteristic in hard the monarchy. These agencies, serving as de facto royal courts, were answerable for registering royal edicts among their one of a type abilties.

The nobility in the parlements perceived their traditional feudal privileges as being endangered within the past due 18th century, leading them to defy the monarch with the resource of the usage of refusing to sign in decrees. These privileges included exemption from various taxes, which the nobles have been resolute in preserving.

Although the parlements were ultimately forced to yield after they clashed with the monarchy, they have been increasingly growing as centers of competition.

In 1778, France decided itself at struggle with Britain, lending assist to the American colonists in their conflict for independence. The fee of the struggle have end up exorbitant, resulting in France amassing huge debt to finance the conflict. Jean Charles Colbert, France's finance minister at the time, proposed a stamp tax and a current land tax in 1787, each levied with out exemptions for the rich. Expecting competition from the parlements, he recommended the king to convene a Council of Notables to planned on the problem, believing that the parlements couldn't dare to protest inside the occasion that they granted their approval.

However, the final effects became sudden. The Assembly of Notables, composed predominantly of nobility and without elections, become determined on with the useful resource of the monarch. Nevertheless, after they convened in 1787, the notables declared themselves powerless to recommend the proposed measures. Instead, they recommended that the king summon the Estates-General, the final time it were convened dating again to 1614.

In June 1787, King Louis XVI disbanded the assembly and registered the brand new tax decrees with the Paris parlement, however as anticipated, no longer one of the legislators affixed their signatures. The assembly became dissolved in August, but through September 1787, the monarch had no preference but to reinstate it. The diploma changed into set for a tumultuous period that could ultimately culminate inside the French Revolution.

The French Revolution Unfolds

As tensions simmered in the route of France, close by assemblies voiced their competition to the king's suggestions and demanded a convocation of the Estates-General. In a momentous selection, the king acquiesced to their desires and summoned the Estates-General in July of 1788.

However, a cloud of tragedy hung over the king and his realm. The rate of bread, the primary sustenance of the impoverished, had surged due to crop disasters in 1787 and 1788, igniting public discontent.

For the number one time for the cause that 1614, the Estates-General convened, divided into 3 awesome estates. The 1/3 property represented the common people, while the second one assets encompassed the clergy, and the primary property represented the aristocracy. However, passing a bill required unanimous help from all three estates, granting the nobility and clergy the electricity to overturn any guidelines enacted thru the 0.33 property.

The 1/three estate, serving because of the truth the voice of the general population, contested this affiliation, deeming it unjust. They encouraged for all Estates-General members to vote simultaneously, with the majority finding out the future of proposed laws. At that component, the zero.33 assets constituted almost half of of the Estates-General representatives. With the beneficial resource of influential human beings of the clergy and nobility, they aimed to enact reforms.

On May 5, 1789, the Estates-General collected to strong their votes. Discord surfaced almost immediately. By June, the zero.33 belongings's staying power wore thin, and they proclaimed themselves the expert representatives of the people of France on June 17, adopting the call "National Assembly." On June 19, the clergy, albeit with the aid of the use of the use of a slender margin, selected to align with the National Assembly.

The King's Dilemma and the Storming of the Bastille

While the monarch and his advisors grew more and more worried, the National Assembly's assertiveness persevered to rise. On Saturday, June 20, 1789, the deputies decided their assembly place sealed and protected via troops. Unyielding, the Third Estate convened at a close-by tennis court docket docket, vowing now not to disband till the king acceded to their needs. On Monday, June 22, a whole lot of the neighborhood clergy rallied to their motive.

Faced with mounting stress, the king ultimately relented on June 27, issuing an edict for the 3 estates to vote collectively. The selection provided a enjoy of remedy to the Parisians and signaled a willingness to interact in reform.

However, the king's next desire to installation his military towards Paris reignited apprehension. Fearful citizens commenced searching for method to guard themselves, main to the raid of the Invalides, a veterans' sanatorium, on the morning of July 14, 1789, wherein they seized its arsenal. Encircling the Bastille, a castle and jail symbolizing royal tyranny, the determined crowd forced the governor to give up. The fall of the Bastille held massive significance, signifying the rejection of royal authority and the sunrise of a today's era.

The Monarch's Eroding Power

As information reached the king that his army's loyalty become questionable, he reconsidered using force. The worry that the troops may also refuse to open fireplace at the populace induced a shift in his stance. The monarchy's grip on energy started out to slide.

In the wake of the Bastille's fall, a ultra-modern municipal administration, led via a discern named Bailly, emerged in Paris. A citizen navy, tasked with maintaining order inside the metropolis, have emerge as formed. Operating beneath Lafayette's command, the National Guard assumed responsibility for making sure peace and balance.

Chapter 5: The Great Fear And The Abolition Of Feudalism

The wave of protest spread all through rural France, an episode called the "Great Fear," or La Grande Peur. The aristocracy have end up accused of conspiring with brigands to retaliate against the commoners, stoking first-rate panic. In their desperation, the commoners abruptly armed themselves, even rebelling in the direction of their landlords whilst the anticipated brigands did now not materialize.

For centuries, the peasants had borne the load of feudal dues to their rulers. Now, they seized manage of feudal tax records and destroyed them, regularly resorting to arson and looting. The National Assembly, recognizing that instant remedy have come to be important to repair peace, took the momentous desire to abolish feudal dues. On the midnight of August four, 1789, the meeting resolved to get rid of the feudal rights held via the French the Aristocracy, marking a huge milestone inside the tumultuous journey of the French Revolution.

With the fervor of revolution sweeping thru France, the National Assembly conventional the Declaration of the Rights of Man and the Citizen on August 26, 1789 this groundbreaking assertion boldly asserted the equality and freedom of everybody. It prohibited arbitrary arrests and detentions, whilst proclaiming that public place of job appointments ought to be completely primarily based on merit, promising equality for all residents.

Despite those modern strides, the French monetary tool persevered to spiral into turmoil. Soaring bread expenses inflicted further worry upon already struggling people.

Amidst these difficult times, a catastrophe spread out on the equal time as King Louis XVI ordered the relocation of infantrymen from the border to his opulent chateau at Versailles. The Parisians, alarmed through this circulate, took matters into their non-public arms on October five, 1789. Large companies of girls seized weapons and cannons, embarking on a march to Versailles. There, they stormed a National Assembly meeting in their pursuit of food or maybe dispatched a delegation to the monarch.

While the ones activities unfold out, the National Guard, led thru Lafayette, made its way to Versailles. Despite Lafayette's preliminary reluctance to go away Paris undefended, mounting stress from his troops forced him to act. Upon his arrival in Versailles, Lafayette "requested" that the king relocate to Paris, a skip that found overwhelming manual a number of the not unusual human beings. Responding to the population's clamor, King Louis XVI consented on October 6, 1789, to transfer his house to the capital.

Restructuring and Reforms

Amid this tumultuous period, the National Assembly initiated remarkable reforms, transforming the panorama of French governance. It disbanded the antique parlements, setting up new courts and dividing France into 80 3 departments, every managed with the aid of the use of way of elected councils. These reforms delivered a today's taxation system to update the vintage one.

The Catholic Church additionally witnessed a giant transformation. Before August four, 1789, citizens had been required to make contributions 10% in their profits to the Church. In November, the Assembly opted to provide the clergy with salaries, effectively making them state employees, and commenced the technique of seizing Church lands.

A committee in the Assembly crafted plans for Church reform, introducing changes to the reimbursement shape and the kind of bishops, with 80 three bishops assigned to the divisions. The church moreover consolidated its parishes, and neighborhood assemblies may henceforth choose parish priests and nearby assemblies ought to vote for their bishops.

In July 1790, the revised designs for Church reform, called the Civil Constitution of the Clergy, had been completed. However, severa people of the clergy were reluctant to cooperate, and in November 1790, the Assembly surpassed a preference to expel any clergy member who refused to take an oath of constancy to the present day day charter. While a few French clerics adhered to the oath, others staunchly resisted and relinquished their positions.

The year 1790 witnessed the emergence of a schism in France among revolutionaries who believed the united states had stepped forward a ways sufficient and those who recommended for similarly radicalization.

The king's ill-fated try to escape France in 1791 handiest exacerbated the kingdom's troubles. On the night time of June 20, the royal family vanished. However, the king's real intentions have come to be smooth even as their royal procession became halted at Varennes. It have become obvious that the monarch did now not guide the revolution and sought to reverse its direction, making King Louis as an opportunity unpopular among French residents.

A New Constitution and Tensions

By September 1791, the present day day constitution come to be entire and bought the monarch's approval. Despite the development, substantial limitations remained. The king retained the authority to pick and dismiss ministers, and balloting rights remained restricted to a pick out part of the male population, except the poorest contributors of society.

The first assembly of the Legislative Assembly took place in October 1791, marking the graduation of a two-twelve months term for the newly fashioned assembly. The assembly's decrees can be overridden with the useful resource of the usage of the king, but handiest finally of the assembly's term, which lasted up to two years.

In April 1792, France located itself plunged into struggle with Austria and, in May of the same 365 days, with Prussia. These army conflicts represented an extreme segment in the French Revolution, first of all marked by means of the usage of using setbacks and big unease, as France confronted ambitious outside demanding conditions, on the equal time as the hazard of internal discord loomed huge.

As the summer season of 1792 unfold out, the French monarchy confronted increasing hostility. Divisions internal Paris had been recommended, every with its very very own assembly. On August nine, power have end up wrested from the ones community assemblies, primary to their unification in the advent of the Commune of Paris. The Commune dispatched national guards to understand the monarch, King Louis XVI, who end up compelled into hiding. The Swiss guards reliable to the king resisted however had been ruthlessly slaughtered.

Following the ones events, the Legislative Assembly announced the king's abdication, rendering the Constitution of 1791, which granted the monarch a large function, unenforceable. In September 1792, the National Convention convened, and the parliament unanimously resolved to hold elections for a new governing frame.

On August 17, 1792, the Commune installed a tribunal to attempt the ones accused of political offenses. Tragically, France witnessed its first political execution via manner of guillotine on August 21.

The dreadful month of September 1792 bore witness to brutal political executions as a weather of paranoia and worry swept over France. The Prussian navy's improve into French territory contributed to this ecosystem of panic. Parisians, fed on thru dread, initiated the bloodbath of political prisoners held in severa metropolis prisons. Kangaroo courts operated, important to the murder of loads. This grim duration of bloodshed in September earned the somber perceive of the "September Massacres."

France's fortunes took a turn even as its military successfully halted the Prussian forces at the Battle of Valmy on August 20, 1792, marking the onset of a modern section within the revolution.

The National Convention, a new governing frame, made a significant decision to terminate the monarchy. The trial of King Louis XVI commenced in December 1792, culminating in his execution on January 15, 1793. Marie Antoinette met the identical future on October 16, 1793.

The repercussions of the king's execution reverberated globally. Britain declared war on France inside the aftermath of the regicide. By February 1793, the French government, determined to hold its warfare strive, instituted compulsory navy service.

Yet, due to the reality the burdens of conscription weighed intently on France, the revolution confronted developing opposition in conservative regions. In March 1793, uprisings erupted in the Vendee and other regions of Brittany, most important to giant bloodshed before the revolt changed into ultimately quelled in December.

The early months of 1793 bore witness to navy defeats and internal uprisings, prompting the mounted order of the Committee for Public Safety in April. This committee functioned as a conflict cabinet throughout the ones tumultuous times.

Another public rise up ensued in Paris in June, important to a purge of the National Convention. Moderate participants, referred to as Girondins, have been expelled, at the same time as radical revolutionaries, the Jacobins, ascended to energy. It grow to be at this juncture that the French Revolution transitioned into its most radical section.

In August, the British effectively captured Toulon, intensifying the navy predicament. To address the dire state of affairs, on August 23, 1793, the government issued a "Levee en Masse," a mounted name to hands.

Concurrently, a greater sinister development unfold out within the form of Watch Committees, hooked up to show strangers and potential threats, emerging in March of 1793. Their authority progressed appreciably in September of the same 12 months, permitting regulation enforcement to detain absolutely everyone recognized as an "enemy of liberty" because of their assist for tyranny, federalism, or different perceived threats. The enormous interpretation of this term resulted in a brutal purge, main to the deaths of as a minimum sixteen,000 individuals within the ensuing 9 months.

Yet, because of the fact the political landscape endured to shift, a glimmer of choice regarded at the navy the front. The Battle of Wattignies in October 1793 marked a turning component as French forces emerged powerful, with Captain Napoleon Bonaparte regaining control of Toulon in December 1793.

Amid those tumultuous times, the Jacobins, lots of whom held atheistic or deistic ideals and harbored disdain for Christianity, spearheaded the De-Christianization motion in September 1793. This resulted in the persecution of the Church, with places of worship forcibly closed and defiled. The iconic Notre Dame Cathedral grow to be rebranded due to the fact the "Temple of Reason."

An crucial symbolic alternate got here in October, changing the very size of time itself. The Christian technology turned into supplanted with the beneficial aid of a new gadget, commencing at the twenty second of September 1792, the number one day of the republic. This new calendar featured one year stimulated with the aid of the herbal international and accompanied a 10-day week, discarding the previous seven-day shape.

However, because the Revolution persisted its tumultuous path, the Convention grew more and more stressful. Fearful of Maximilien Robespierre's functionality for arbitrary arrests and executions, they determined to act decisively. On the 27th of July, Robespierre tried to quit his own lifestyles, exceptional to be apprehended and completed day after today, the twenty 8th of July, 1794.

With Robespierre's fall from strength, the units of fear that had gripped the state commenced to resolve, primary to the release of severa incarcerated individuals.

In March 1795, numerous church homes, which had remained closed to worship considering October 1793, had been sooner or later allowed to reopen.

By August of 1794, the Convention had finalized a brand new charter. This charter brought a -chamber device of presidency in France. The government authority come to be vested inside the five-member body referred to as the Directory, signaling a few one-of-a-kind shift in the u.S.A.'s political panorama. Additionally, the National Guard and sectional assemblies have been dissolved in October 1794, bringing approximately further adjustments as France continued its tumultuous adventure via the modern technology.

In the overdue 18th century, the Directory's earnest endeavors to restore peace and stability to the government of France proved elusive. The year 1799 witnessed a rustic yearning for tranquility and protection, and it end up for the duration of those turbulent times that the charismatic discern of Napoleon Bonaparte emerged as a beacon of wish. His decisive movement to quell a Parisian rebellion in September 1795, known as the 'whiff of grapeshot,' thrust him into the limelight. In the following years, from 1796 to 1797, he orchestrated a successful advertising marketing campaign in the course of the Austrians in Northern Italy, incomes accolades and the popularity of a country huge hero.

Napoleon's military prowess prolonged to the Egyptian advertising and marketing and advertising advertising and marketing campaign, spanning from 1798 to 1799. Although he performed substantial victories on land, the French army suffered a devastating blow inside the Battle of the Nile in 1798.

In October 1799, Napoleon lower back to France and spearheaded a coup d'état the subsequent month, ushering in a present day generation postdating the French Revolution.

Chapter 6: France Inside The 19th Century

Initially assuming the call of "First Consul," Napoleon's dominion have become undisputed. A new charter, popularly encouraged, consolidated his authority, predominant to his appointment as consul for a ten-one year time period. In 1802, each different referendum expanded him to an entire life characteristic, and, in 1804, Napoleon topped himself emperor.

While Napoleon retained severa of the current necessities established in France, permitting individuals to pursue careers based totally on ability and competence without discrimination, he delivered press manipulate and trial-by manner of-jury incarceration. A centralized administration underneath prefects grow to be instituted to manipulate the numerous departments.

Despite his progressive reforms, Napoleon curtailed women's rights and reinstated slavery within the French colonies for the duration of his rule. In 1801, he reached a concordat settlement with the Pope, and, in 1804, he promulgated the Code Napoleon, an entire set of prison pointers governing the French kingdom.

In parallel with the ones home guidelines, Napoleon's strategic brilliance enabled him to dominate a whole lot of Europe. A coalition of Austria, Russia, and Britain normal in 1799 to oppose France, however Russia withdrew its useful resource in 1800, fundamental to Austria's capitulation in the following 365 days. Although Britain declared peace in 1802, hostilities resumed in 1803.

In 1804, a third coalition, comprising Russia, Austria, and Britain, changed into forged, but Napoleon's tactical acumen secured a decisive victory on the Battle of Austerlitz in 1805. The 12 months 1806 witnessed Prussia's get admission to into the conflict, however their defeat at Jena marked the cease in their resistance.

However, no matter Napoleon's amazing efforts, the French and Spanish fleets suffered a powerful defeat in October 1805 at the Battle of Trafalgar. Napoleon remained ascendant till 1812 even as the tide commenced to reveal. Following his disastrous invasion of Russia, Prussia declared struggle on France in 1813. The Battle of Leipzig in October 1813 noticed Austria and Sweden be part of the coalition, fundamental to a decisive defeat of the French forces.

The allied invasion of Paris in March 1814 pressured Napoleon to abdicate, and he have grow to be subsequently exiled to the island of Elba. However, he staged a dramatic return to France in 1815, to start with welcomed with the resource of the population. Yet, in June, he met his Waterloo and become compelled to abdicate once more, this time being despatched to St. Helena, wherein he breathed his very last in 1821.

Following Napoleon's exile, his brother Louis XVIII ascended to the throne. Despite the sooner loss of life of Louis XVI in 1793, his son, who royalists believed need to be topped

Louis XVII, had handed away in 1795. Recognizing the impossibility of completely reversing the clock, Louis XVIII accredited France to embody a constitution.

In an try and rein inside the Ultra-royalists, who sought to obliterate the remnants of the revolution, Louis XVIII's reign come to be marred with the beneficial aid of the assassination of the Duc de Berry in 1820, which reinforced the power of the hardline royalists.

Upon Louis XVIII's loss of life in 1824, Charles X ascended to the throne. Charles, maintaining divine proper to rule, resisted negotiations with liberals, leading to an rise up in 1830 and his next deposition.

Fearing ability violence from neighboring worldwide places in reaction to a republican recognition quo, the French populace hesitated to adopt this form of device. Instead, Louis Philippe, Duc d'Orleans, assumed the throne and presided over an 18-one year reign. During his rule, the French

Constitution have turn out to be greater progressive, extending the proper to vote to a broader segment of the center splendor, on the same time as people even though remained excluded from the franchise.

Amidst the reign of Charles X, the French ventured into the territory of Algeria, marking the commencement of a prolonged conquest that persisted thru Louis Philippe's rule. The way, however, changed into a long one.

While France did experience the nascent stirrings of the economic revolution, the tempo of industrialization within the nation lagged behind the short changes witnessed in countries like Britain and Germany. Agriculture remained the dominant financial interest. Nevertheless, thru 1848, numerous towns were teeming with town employee's toiling in deplorable situations and increasingly more advocated thru socialist thoughts.

The "July Monarchy" beneath Louis Philippe proved to be a trifling period in-between, as big discontent and a immoderate financial downturn rocked France in 1846 and 1847.

Finally, in February 1848, a big protest erupted in Paris. Tragically, the reaction of infantrymen beginning fireplace on demonstrators brought on a speedy revolution. Louis Philippe abdicated his throne and fled the scene.

To alleviate unemployment and pacify public anger, temporary government mounted country wide workshops in Paris, attracting jobless people from the nation-state. However, humans' discontent persisted, fundamental to ongoing protests. In June 1848, the government resolved to shut the workshops and disperse the hard work pressure. Nevertheless, employees remained undeterred, erecting barricades in a few unspecified time in the future of Paris. The authorities forces sooner or later quelled the rebellion, referred to as the June Days.

The new constitution changed into unveiled to the general public in November 1848, permitting all eligible males to sturdy their votes and choose out a unified legislature and president. In December 1848, the nephew of Napoleon Bonaparte, Louis Napoleon, secured the presidency.

Nonetheless, the constitution prohibited the President from attempting to find a 2nd term, prompting Louis Napoleon to diploma a coup on December 2, 1851. The people advocated the go along with the glide, granting the president the authority to regulate the constitution, and Louis Napoleon assumed the discover of emperor in December 1852.

Napoleon III modified into instrumental inside the revitalization of Paris in the course of his rule, overseeing the improvement of spacious boulevards and the implementation of a contemporary sewage device, reworking the town into a more healthy city. The creation business enterprise additionally supplied employment for lots.

Simultaneously, France persisted its industrialization efforts, developing its railway network and putting in place new banks inside the path of Napoleon's reign.

However, Napoleon's foreign places coverage pursuits were in big element marked with the resource of the usage of failure. In 1854, he engaged in the Crimean War in the direction of Russia, which yielded little gain for France with the aid of its result in 1856. In 1859, France waged struggle towards Austria, emerging a fulfillment however with meager rewards.

In 1862, Britain and Spain initiated an tour to Mexico to get better a debt, with France later becoming a member of the try. Despite the withdrawal of Britain and Spain, Napoleon erroneously attempted to put in the Austrian prince Maximilian as emperor of Mexico. A citizen insurrection in Mexico precipitated Napoleon to withdraw his forces in 1865, with Maximilian ultimately going through a firing squad.

Napoleon's reputation waned after 1867, leading him to enact greater liberal rules, which encompass loosening press restrictions and permitting political rallies with decreased oversight. Workers had been granted the proper to strike.

Nonetheless, in 1870, Napoleon's unwell-fated choice to salary warfare in opposition to Prussia culminated in a effective French defeat at Sedan in September. Napoleon have come to be in the long run overthrown and captured, in the long run departing the u . S ..

Adolphe Thiers assumed control of a provisional management, at the same time as Paris confronted dire meals shortages as German forces laid siege to the metropolis. Finally, on January 28, 1871, Paris capitulated, resulting within the loss of Alsace and Lorraine within the peace agreement. German troops remained stationed in northern France until France paid an indemnity.

In the wake of Paris's tumultuous fall, a National Assembly hastily assumed authority, convening within the regal environment of Versailles. However, the peace agreement that transpired from the battle left Parisians brimming with fury, prompting a vehement rebel.

Under the banner of the Commune, the Parisians established their very very very own municipal control, defiant inside the face of adversity. Thiers, at the helm of the essential authorities, grow to be decided in quelling the rise up. Consequently, on May 21, 1871, he dispatched the troops, and the French forces methodically superior thru the town, block with the aid of manner of block, to regain manipulate, ensuing in extremely good casualties.

Subsequent to his election as president, Thiers expeditiously attended to Germany's repayment claims. By September 1873, all German troops were withdrawn from French soil.

Meanwhile, Marshal MacMahon, a staunch monarchist, succeeded Thiers as president in 1873. Nonetheless, in 1875, the National

Assembly voted in pick of organising the Third Republic.

France's industrialization continued unabated into the past due nineteenth century, with big boom found in the iron and chemical sectors. The early twentieth century witnessed the emergence of the automobile employer as a awesome economic player, determined through the enlargement of the railroad network.

The prevent of the nineteenth century delivered progressed living necessities and nutritional conduct for the common French citizen. Legislative measures enacted in 1900 positioned a cap of 10 hours at the workday for girls and minors.

Yet, on October 15, 1894, Captain Alfred Dreyfus, a member of the French navy's General Staff engaged in intelligence work, became arrested on expenses of treason, accused of promoting sensitive navy statistics to the Germans. Dreyfus have come to be subjected to a responsible verdict and a lifestyles sentence.

However, it have end up evident that Dreyfus end up a sufferer of anti-Semitism, notably talking because of his Jewish historical beyond. His Alsatian historical beyond moreover marked him as an outsider. In reality, Dreyfus have grow to be harmless of the allegations.

Two years later, Lieutenant Colonel Georges Picquart exposed proof that pointed to Major Walsin Esterhazy due to the fact the real wrongdoer. Despite the compelling proof, the navy transferred Picquart to Tunisia and a navy court docket docket acquitted Esterhazy.

In a pivotal newspaper article titled "J'accuse!" (I accuse), authored with the useful resource of Emile Zola, the duvet-up thru way of the army became exposed. This divisive case cleaved French society, with the right-wing factions and the top echelons of the Catholic Church siding in opposition to

Dreyfus, at the same time as the left-wing segments staunchly supported his purpose.

In 1899, Dreyfus confronted a 2nd court-martial, resulting in but some different accountable verdict. However, he turn out to be in the end granted a pardon through the president and approved to move returned to France. It end up not till 1906 that Dreyfus's name modified into sooner or later cleared, securing his exoneration.

Twentieth-Century France

The 12 months 1906 witnessed the formal enactment of a statute officially placing apart Church and nation.

Then, in 1914, France, along aspect the relaxation of Europe, emerge as thrust into the vortex of the First World War. During the protracted warfare, France incurred the lack of about 1.Three million infantrymen, with kind of 1,000,000 greater maimed. The conflict inflicted a huge toll at the French financial gadget, ensuing in significant property damage, loss of farm animals, and the accumulation of widespread country wide debt.

Nonetheless, the Twenties heralded an monetary revival for France. By 1924, industrial output had rebounded to fit the levels of 1914, sooner or later surging by means of manner of forty percent in 1929. An influx of migrants, which encompass Poles, Italians, and Spaniards, attempting to find employment, similarly invigorated the French personnel.

However, the worldwide economic calamity added about by using the 1929 Wall Street Crash in the long run affected France's financial trajectory, albeit with a now not on time onset, beginning in 1932.

Amidst the turbulence of the Nineteen Thirties, the Communist and Socialist factions placed common ground. The 1936 elections culminated within the victory of a coalition called the Popular Front. Subsequently, a wave of actions and place of business occupations ensued, leading to an accord amongst major employers and the Popular Front's leader, Leon Blum.

Known because the Matignon Accord, it led to a 10% sales growth, the repute quo of a 40-hour workweek, and weeks of paid excursion for employees. Nevertheless, the French economic machine remained gradual, and unemployment costs remained stepped forward.

On September three, 1939, France declared conflict on Germany, marking the wonderful commencement of World War II.

In May 1940, German forces released an invasion of unbiased Holland and Belgium. In response, French and British troops advanced into Belgium to counter the invasion. However, German tanks pierced the Ardennes Forest in northeastern France, efficaciously encircling the Allied forces.

As the dark clouds of World War II loomed over France, over one hundred forty,000

French squaddies, alongside aspect the British army, launched right into a deadly journey inside the route of the seas. By that time, German forces had made massive inroads into France, and the u . S . A . Bore witness to tens of millions of terrified residents fleeing in each possible route. Ultimately, on June 22, 1940, France would possibly formally surrender to the German forces.

The terms imposed thru the Germans had been stringent, leaving the French military extensively depleted, with an insignificant 100,000 soldiers available because of the German profession of the northern and japanese areas. The French parliament, responding to the dire scenario, granted Marshal Petain dictatorial powers on July 10, 1940. This marked the inception of a modern-day fascist country, with Vichy serving as its capital. Swiftly, the Vichy manipulate brought anti-Semitic suggestions, no matter the fact that their rule might be brief-lived, as German forces overran southern France in November 1942.

The German career of France discovered the united states's sources systematically tired. Thousands of French residents were forcibly despatched to Germany to feature worker's, and the Germans pillaged the u . S . A .'s agricultural output and enterprise gadgets, resulting in sizeable starvation and deprivation for the duration of France.

Amidst the turmoil, General Charles de Gaulle assumed command of French forces that continued to withstand the German profession from their base in England. Meanwhile, resistance businesses took form inner France.

It wasn't till the summer time of 1944 that the Allies liberated France, with de Gaulle ultimately assuming the characteristic of meantime president. However, with the aid of manner of January 1946, a dispute with the newly elected legislature brought approximately de Gaulle's resignation.

In 1947, France followed a trendy constitution. De Gaulle remained a vocal opponent of this charter, as he had foreseen that it would herald a chain of vain governments. Nevertheless, through the late 1940s, France had made a extraordinary positioned up-warfare recovery, and in 1951, French commercial output ultimately caught up to its pre-struggle levels.

Yet, the French colonies ought to pose annoying conditions within the Nineteen Fifties. France's considerable colonial empire in Southeast Asia, installation toward the forestall of the nineteenth century, modified into marred by using growing needs for autonomy, mainly in Vietnam. In a pivotal turning element, the French have been defeated via the Communists in Dien Bien Phu in 1954, main to their withdrawal from Vietnam.

Internal divisions in France have been further exacerbated thru the contentious problem of Algerian independence. On May thirteen, 1958, French colonists in Algeria staged a coup, raising the risk of civil conflict in France.

Amidst this catastrophe, the National Assembly, on June 1, 1958, granted de Gaulle emergency powers for a six-month period, correctly terminating the Fourth Republic.

The Fifth Republic in France

In September 1958, de Gaulle called for a vote on a state-of-the-art charter, which garnered overwhelming help from the French population. Consequently, de Gaulle consolidated significant presidential authority into his personal fingers.

De Gaulle initiated negotiations with the Front de Liberation Nationale (FLN) in Algeria in 1959. In opposition to independence, French colonists in Algeria common the Organisation de l'Armée Secrète (OAS) in 1961. Despite assassination attempts on de Gaulle, Algeria voted for independence in July 1962.

De Gaulle, although re-elected in 1965, secured a slim majority within the election. However, in May 1968, France descended into chaos. The scholar protests that started out at the University of Nanterre unexpectedly unfold, engulfing the Sorbonne. These demonstrations had been now not restricted to college students, as personnel, too, joined the dissent. The subsequent brutal response of riot police to the protestors on May 10 induced sizeable moves referred to as thru way of exchange unions. The protests even spilled into the French nation-state.

Remarkably, inside the course of the tumultuous period, the Communist Party remained supportive of de Gaulle. Prime Minister Georges Pompidou attempted to placate the running beauty with the useful resource of imparting income will increase. When de Gaulle in the end known as for elections, a right-wing backlash ensued, quelling the catastrophe in France. Nevertheless, de Gaulle selected to step down in 1969, and he handed away in 1970.

Pompidou succeeded de Gaulle due to the fact the president of France, prevailing reelection in 1972, despite the reality that his tenure have become reduce short through his next passing. Valery Giscard d'Estaing assumed the presidency and, in 1972, France adopted the Euro.

Francois Mitterrand took workplace due to the fact the president of France in 1981. Mitterrand, a socialist, expanded the welfare nation and decreased the art work hours required for benefits. However, the dream abruptly soured, with inflation and unemployment surging in the early 1980s, necessitating repeated devaluations of the franc.

Mitterrand in the long run reversed direction, imposing pay freezes and trimming government fees. By 1986, inflation had receded, and while unemployment remained excessive, it remained robust. In 1988, Mitterrand changed into re-elected, however Jacques Chirac assumed the presidency In 1995. Concurrently, in 1999, France accompanied the Euro.

Chapter 7: Contemporary France

In the 365 days 2002, a pivotal second within the history of France end up marked through a political alliance that aimed to make certain the reelection of Jacques Chirac. The Rally for the Republic (RPR) joined forces with unique events, developing the center-right Union for the Presidential Majority. This alliance, later renamed the Union for a Popular Movement (UMP), had a unique goal: to maintain Chirac's grip at the presidency. The collaboration bore fruit as Chirac convincingly triumphed over the a long way-right candidate, Le Pen. The latter's excellent overall general overall performance in the first spherical of the elections had pressured Lionel Jospin to withdraw from the race.

With the Socialists out of the photograph, Chirac seized the opportunity to lease fellow Gaullist Jean-Pierre Raffarin due to the fact the top minister. However, the intricacies of the French political landscape remained as they have been – a sensitive balancing act among cutting-edge social policies and the disturbing situations posed with the resource of immoderate taxes, arduous social safety burdens on organizations, and the precarious financing of health and welfare packages.

The 12 months 2003 delivered global hobby to France while the Chirac management took a company stand in opposition to the authorization of the usage of strain in Iraq. This stance led several contributors of the United Nations Security Council to believe that Saddam Hussein's regime became truly cooperating with weapons inspectors. Despite giant manual for Chirac's feature on Iraq many of the French populace, the UMP faced setbacks in every close by and European Parliament elections that 12 months.

Chirac's reputation suffered some other blow inside the following 365 days while French residents rejected the approval of a ultra-modern European Union constitution, a motive he had championed. In the wake of this failure, Chirac appointed Dominique de Villepin, one in every of his proteges, as the brand new high minister, selecting him over his long-time rival, Nicolas Sarkozy, who assumed the position of UMP leader and moreover took price of the indoors ministry.

The year 2005 witnessed a large turning factor at the same time as the accidental deaths of two immigrant youths in Paris ignited riots that rapid spread in the path of the u . S .. French pride in the u . S .'s variety began out to wane as immoderate unemployment, prejudice, and a loss of possibilities maximum of the predominantly North African immigrant populace fueled the unrest. The fall riots resulted in the destruction of approximately 9,000 motors and the detention of sincerely 3,000 people.

In 2006, over 1,000,000 humans throughout the dominion set up in the direction of a proposed bill that aimed to make it less complicated to terminate the employment of younger employees, similarly underscoring the overall public's dissatisfaction with the management. With Chirac's recognition plummeting, he had no preference but to rapid slump the regulation.

The Government Under Sarkozy

As the twelve months 2007 approached, Chirac may also need to have sought reelection as president underneath the French constitution, but he decided on not to. The most essential political activities inside the u.S.A. Nominated relative beginners to be successful him, reflecting the public's preference for change. Nicolas Sarkozy effects secured the candidacy of the center-right UMP, even as the Socialist Party determined on Ségolène Royal, an extended-time aide to François Mitterrand. Both applicants advanced to the runoff election, with Sarkozy in the end growing because the victor. Royal made records because the first lady to attain this diploma. Critics unfairly in assessment Sarkozy to an American neoconservative, at the same time as his supporters applauded his plans to reduce unemployment, decrease taxes, streamline authorities operations, and impose stricter penalties for unlawful immigration.

By the only yr 2010, discontent with Sarkozy and the UMP had grown due to excessive unemployment and economic instability. The UMP accomplished poorly in close by elections in March, principal the Socialist Party and its allies to take control of 21 of the usa of a's 22 areas. A nationwide strike and incredible protests erupted in France that summer season in reaction to proposed austerity measures, in particular a plan to raise the retirement age.

Additional actions that fall delivered hundreds of hundreds of human beings into the streets and wreaked havoc on the u.S.'s transportation device. Sarkozy confronted more criticism for the expulsion of loads of Romanians and Bulgarians, the bulk of whom were Roma (Gypsies) dwelling in unlawful camps, drawing condemnation from the European Union.

In July, the French decrease residence held a vote that triggered the unanimous adoption of regulation in September 2010, which banned face-concealing clothing in public regions. While the law did now not explicitly factor out Islamic garb, it have come to be notably interpreted as pertaining to complete-face veils. Offenders confronted €a hundred fifty fines as soon as the law got here into impact in April 2011.

Conflict inside the Eurozone and the Rise of the Socialists

In the early years of the 21st century, France decided itself at the coronary heart of a turbulent Europe, grappling with the continuing Eurozone debt catastrophe. These hard instances set the diploma for a large shift in French politics. As the united states of the us braced for the 2012 presidential election, a handful of outstanding contenders emerged, every vying for the coveted characteristic.

Marine Le Pen, together together with her charismatic populist appeal, brief surged in the race after assuming manage of the National Front, succeeding her father. Simultaneously, many had predicted that Dominique Strauss-Kahn, the Director of the International Monetary Fund, may turn out to be the Socialist Party's nominee. However, his political aspirations have been all of sudden derailed at the same time as he faced sexual assault allegations in New York City in May 2011, causing his rapid fall from attention.

Several months later, whilst the prices in the direction of Strauss-Kahn have been disregarded, it modified into too late for the Socialists, who had already rallied in the returned of François Hollande, their former leader, as their new desired-bearer. Amidst these political shifts, Nicolas Sarkozy, who had served because the president of the Group of Eight and the Group of 20, labored intently with German Chancellor Angela Merkel in an attempt to combat the economic crisis that loomed over Europe.

Sarkozy's tenure as president have been marked via domestic monetary suggestions geared closer to curtailing the French fee variety deficit. However, the ones measures little by little eroded his reputation. The authorities faced an sudden setback in September 2011 even as the Socialist Party and its allies secured a majority inside the Senate, marking the first time the Socialists had received such manipulate in the pinnacle chamber because the fame quo of the Fifth Republic in 1958, with its system of oblique elections.

Chapter 8: The Government Underneath Hollande

In October 2011, France witnessed its first-ever open primary election, and François Hollande emerged because of the truth the effective candidate, securing the Socialist nomination. He then confronted off against 9 one-of-a-kind contenders inside the first spherical of the presidential election in April 2012. Hollande's achievement in taking pics over 18% of the vote, securing a stable 1/three-area cease, changed right into a large success. Marine Le Pen, the leader of the National Front, made data through important her birthday celebration to a record-breaking result, setting up herself as a effective political pressure.

Sarkozy trailed inside the once more of Hollande, setting the extent for a runoff. Over the following weeks, Sarkozy fervently courted supporters of the National Front, spotting their pivotal feature in his electoral prospects. On May 6, 2012, François Hollande made records because the first Socialist president thinking about the reality that François Mitterrand's victory over Jacques Chirac in 1988. He secured about fifty percentage of the vote. Following his presidential triumph, the Socialists clinched 314 seats within the National Assembly, granting them a commanding supermajority within the decrease chamber of presidency without a doubt one month later.

Although Marine Le Pen narrowly omitted victory in her marketing campaign for a legislative seat, different National Front applicants effectively again the birthday party to the parliament for the number one time considering that 1997.

Hollande, alongside together with his points of interest set on monetary increase, wasted no time in enforcing numerous home advertising and marketing campaign pledges upon taking place of work. He delivered a arguable seventy five% tax on earnings exceeding €1,000,000, or approximately $1,three hundred,000, and multiplied

France's withdrawal from the NATO operation in Afghanistan. While the "millionaires' tax" became in the long run invalidated by France's Constitutional Court in December 2012, Hollande remained devoted to resubmitting the revised tax invoice, given its popularity maximum of the French population.

Hollande's presidency faced mounting challenges due to the fact the unemployment charge in France soared past 10%, and his approval ratings step by step declined. His seasoned-business improvement duties alienated his leftist allies, while his tax pointers drew the ire of his right-wing critics. In March 2013, he unveiled a changed version of the "millionaires' tax," shifting its cognizance from human beings to agencies. Furthermore, the National Assembly passed a groundbreaking regulation allowing same-intercourse marriage and granting same-sex couples the proper to adopt on April 23, 2013.

Despite Hollande's unwavering dedication to enhancing France's monetary situation, the country continued to grapple with economic fragility. Although the financial machine showed signs of a gradual recuperation, developing unemployment charges strong a shadow over the opportunity of a jobless healing. In the arena of foreign insurance, Hollande maintained a steadfast course, even as his home financial time desk faced setbacks.

In January 2014, French forces released a army intervention in Mali, and in December 2013, they prolonged their involvement to the Central African Republic. Amidst those international worrying situations, Hollande took a resolute stand, urging Western army engagement within the Syrian Civil War following the deployment of chemical guns in a rebellion-held area outside of Damascus. Despite uncertain useful aid from the USA and Britain, Hollande championed a diplomatic method that in the end added about the dismantling of Syria's chemical weapons.

The "Hollande doctrine," aimed to raise France's repute the world over, confronted a lack of well-known help, as showed through the usage of the nearby elections held in March 2014. The Socialists of Hollande suffered a substantial defeat, with the National Front and the Union for a Popular Movement (UMP) winning severa mayorships and close by council seats. Voter apathy amongst Socialist supporters precipitated record-low participation, on the equal time because the National Front's ongoing rebranding contributed to its first-rate-ever election overall performance.

In response, President Hollande reshuffled his authorities, converting Prime Minister Jean-Marc Ayrault with Interior Minister Manuel Valls, a moderate whose now and again controversial mind determined decide on some of the French proper. In the European Parliament election in May, the National Front endured its upward fashion, garnering the most assist.

By July 2014, the unemployment fee in France had risen to almost eleven percentage, and Prime Minister Valls confronted inner dissent interior his government. Economic Minister Arnaud Montebourg, who championed a increase-focused software program over austerity, emerge as disregarded in August 2014 for openly opposing Hollande's financial method. After Valls's cupboard resigned, President Hollande tasked him with developing a trendy management.

During this time, Hollande's reputation declined, on the same time because the UMP faced inner problems that hindered its capacity to capitalize at the president's unpopularity. In an try to revive the struggling birthday party and make a political comeback, Nicolas Sarkozy efficiently received the manage of the UMP at a celebration conference in November 2014.

Tragedy struck in January 2015 while gunmen stormed the Paris headquarters of the satirical mag Charlie Hebdo, ensuing in the deaths of twelve humans. The magazine have become believed to have been centered due to its depictions of the Prophet Muhammad, marking one of the worst terrorist assaults in France in over five a few years. World leaders condemned the assaults, and residents during France amassed in help of the patients. The suspects, brothers with ties to radical Islamist businesses diagnosed to U.S. And French government, sought shelter in a printing facility northeast of Paris on January nine.

They later engaged in a war of words with the police. Simultaneously, every other shooter, claiming association with a larger group, held hostages in a kosher grocery hold in Paris. This man or woman become favored for the murder of a police officer in Montrouge. After severa hours, French protection personnel raided each locations, resulting in the deaths of all three militants internal. The hostage at the printing production facility turn out to be efficiently rescued, despite the fact that there have been four fatalities and almost a dozen hostage rescues at the grocery keep.

On November 13, 2015, a coordinated terrorist assault passed off in and round Paris, resulting inside the deaths of as a minimum 129 people and severa accidents. The attackers used computerized rifles and bomb belts. This was the bloodiest terrorist assault in Europe for the cause that train bombings in Madrid in 2004. President Hollande turn out to be present at the Stade de France inside the Paris network of Saint-Denis at the same time as 3 assailants blew themselves up outside the stadium in the direction of a match among France and Germany.

Islamist extremists moreover opened fireplace on Parisian cafes and ingesting places in the tenth and 11th arrondissements, claiming many lives. At the Bataclan live basic overall performance corridor, 3 gunmen stormed the venue as American rock band Eagles of Death Metal performed for a supplied-out target market, primary to the deaths of as a minimum 89 people.

French police finally raided the Bataclan after extra than hours, at some point of which the attackers held hostages and shot survivors of the preliminary bloodbath. Two of the terrorists detonated their explosive belts, whilst the zero.33 become killed through way of the police. President Hollande declared that France turn out to be "at war" with the Islamic State in Iraq and the Levant (ISIL), commonly known as ISIS, which claimed duty for the assaults.

Over a hundred,000 protection officials were deployed, and an intensive look for ability collaborators happened in France and Belgium inside the days following the attacks. Additionally, French military forces accomplished airstrikes on ISIL-held territories in Syria and Iraq.

On Bastille Day, July 14, 2016, a sad incident unfold out in Nice, as a truck plowed into crowds of human beings celebrating, resulting inside the lack of at least eighty 4 lives and leaving loads injured. This marked the zero.33 most crucial terrorist occasion in France in the previous 18 months. At the time of the attack, tens of hundreds had been dispersing from the Promenade des Anglais alongside the seafront, in which that they'd gathered to experience a fireworks display. The truck traveled almost kilometers alongside the prom earlier than crashing through limitations and right into a pedestrian area. The purpose pressure, a career crook with out a connections to terrorist corporations, modified into killed in a gun war with the police.

President Hollande, without a doubt hours previous to the assault, had expressed his purpose to save you the united states of emergency imposed due to the reality the November 2015 assaults. However, within the wake of this tragedy, he prolonged the kingdom of emergency for a further 3 months and referred to as up the kingdom's army reserves.

As President Hollande's popularity diminished to unmarried digits, he made the selection not to are seeking for reelection in December 2016. Shortly thereafter, Prime Minister Manuel Valls, a member of Hollande's manipulate, resigned and declared his candidacy for the presidential election as a Socialist. Meanwhile, the Republicans (previously the UMP) rejected Nicolas Sarkozy's go again, successfully finishing his opportunities for a political comeback. Sarkozy finished 1/three inside the November Republican number one for president.

François Fillon, Sarkozy's predecessor as immoderate minister, and a representative of conservative French provincial Roman Catholics, emerged due to the fact the victor inside the election. According to polls, Marine Le Pen of the National Front (now National Rally) changed into the most in all likelihood opponent in the presidential runoff in May 2017.

In March 2017, Fillon and his partner faced costs related to the misappropriation of about $1 million in public budget, main to the disintegrate of his candidacy. Le Pen, former Communist Party presidential contender Jean-Luc Mélenchon, and Hollande's finance secretary Emmanuel Macron correctly became the presidential marketing marketing campaign proper into a 3-way battle amongst outsider applicants.

In April 2016, Macron released his political birthday celebration, En Marche!, with a platform paying homage to former British Prime Minister Tony Blair's "1/3 way" beliefs. While Mélenchon and Le Pen appealed to the a ways left and a protracted way proper of the primary activities, respectively, Macron succeeded in prevailing over moderates, inclusive of former immoderate ministers Manuel Valls of the Socialist Party and Alain Juppé of the UMP.

Chapter 9: The Macron Presidency

In April 2017, the primary round of the French presidential election befell, and for the primary time under the Fifth Republic, neither of the 2 important occasions superior to the runoff. Despite final-minute net statistics leaks, attributed to the equal Russian hackers who had tried to persuade the 2016 U.S. Presidential election and referred to as "MacronLeaks," it had no bearing on the final final consequences. Both Macron and Le Pen advanced to the runoff election on May 7. Macron secured a effective victory over Le Pen, turning into the youngest leader of France at the same time as you consider that Napoleon. Macron's En Marche! Done a large triumph in the legislative elections the subsequent month, triumphing 350 out of 577 seats, in alliance with François Bayrou's Democratic Movement (MoDem). Although the election found a file type of women elected to the National Assembly (39%), it became marred through the use of low voter turnout, the bottom in a French legislative election thinking about that World War II.

Emmanuel Macron swiftly rose as a fantastic determine in worldwide politics. Despite his surprising alignment with U.S. President Donald Trump, he stood corporation in his dedication to uphold the Paris Climate Agreement and the Iran nuclear deal. However, Macron's developing global have an effect on did no longer ameliorate his home status. He earned the moniker "president of the rich" (le président des riches) due to his tax guidelines favoring France's wealthiest residents to attract foreign places investments.

In November 2018, large public protests erupted as a response to a planned gas tax increase, main to extraordinary complaint of Macron. He ultimately needed to backpedal on the gasoline tax because of robust public aid for the demonstrators, called the "yellow vests" after the colourful website online traffic protection vests they wore. In April 2019, while a fire severely broken Notre Dame Cathedral in Paris, the public rallied inside the lower returned of Macron, who pledged to rebuild the cathedral and initiated a fundraising marketing and marketing campaign that garnered loads of plenty and thousands of euros.

The global fitness crisis posed via the SARS-CoV-2 pandemic speedy shifted Macron's attention from his time desk to reduce authorities spending. France's economic system gotten smaller appreciably as non-important groups had been close down, and tour emerge as limited. However, america of the us rebounded rapidly, manner to its immoderate vaccination rate and robust technique retention software, stopping the high mortality fees and persistent unemployment witnessed in one-of-a-kind global locations, regardless of over 25 million times of the probable deadly virus in France.

Macron's Perseverance

Macron's reputation remained fairly stagnant at round 40%, notwithstanding his management's commendable managing of the epidemic. The 2021 close by elections, mirroring his poor poll scores, found the disturbing situations he confronted. While the Republicans and Socialists made earnings on a country huge scale, En Marche! Experienced losses during the board. Voter turnout hit some different rock backside, with truely 35% of eligible citizens taking element inside the election.

Facing Apathy

As Macron ready for the 2022 presidential marketing marketing campaign, he struggled to rally his dwindling supporters in the face of huge voter apathy. On April 10, 2022, the number one spherical of voting spread out, bearing a putting resemblance to the 2017 race. Macron secured kind of 28% of the vote, whilst Le Pen trailed with 23%.

Jean-Luc Mélenchon, completing in 0.33 region with 22% of the vote, referred to as on his lovers to withhold their votes from Marine Le Pen. Macron emerged successful within the April 24 runoff, claiming over 58% of the vote and securing a second time period.

Continued Influence

Macron's have an effect on on the European level persisted, and he endeavored to mediate amongst Moscow and Kyiv all through Russia's invasion of Ukraine. However, his domestic reputation failed to see a fantastic growth following his reelection. In the June 2022 elections, his mild alliance out of place its majority within the National Assembly.

Macron opted to reject the resignation of Prime Minister Élisabeth Borne, emphasizing the need for his cupboard to "stay on mission and act." Borne in the long run passed a vote of self assure the following month, whilst Macron discovered himself main a minority control after failing to attract competition events to his alliance.

Pension Reform

In a glide to push a budget diploma via with out the approval of the National Assembly, Macron resorted to invoking Article 40 nine.Three of the French constitution in October 2022. This article, included within the constitution of the Fifth Republic (installed in 1958), end up supposed to shield the president's authority. However, its utilization, which correctly allowed the president to bypass the legislature, had been a rarity, generally employed in instances of minority or break up ("cohabitation") administrations.

Its invocation confronted large grievance as being undemocratic. In March 2023, Macron all over again hired Article forty 9.Three to pass a contentious pension reform package deal deal, which steadily raised the retirement age from sixty to sixty four by using the use of using 2030. Despite going through votes of no self warranty in his manipulate, Macron succeeded in making the pension reform plan into regulation.

Chapter 10: The Top 10 Reasons To Visit France

History, Beauty, And More

France's charming beauty cannot be unnoticed. Even in case you've never been to France in advance than, it has loads to provide. It might absolutely lead you down the direction of nostalgia. It conjures up you with images of the Paris Eiffel Tower, the Cannes Film Festival, Nice's pebbly seashores, Bordeaux's great wines, and Lyon's lovable architecture. While 1/2 of of the area is already in love with France, there are tens of millions of motives why you need to be as nicely. So, right here are 5 actual motives to visit France so that you can also convince your gang, partner, or family to p.C. Their baggage and go to fulfill your excursion thirst.

France by no means fails to wow site visitors together with her particular beauty, paintings, records, and gourmet legacy. That is why it is the maximum well-known visitor internet internet website within the global. Whether you visit France for a severe cause or absolutely to have fun, France offers a few aspect for every body, this is why those "10 Reasons to Visit France" are compelling enough to entice without a doubt absolutely everyone.

1. France is Home to Paris.

Paris is the capital of France. This function by myself should be enough to persuade you to select France above some other region you're considering. Paris is the most adorable metropolis, and no special city can healthful its life, which is nearly great. With iconic internet sites similar to the Eiffel Tower and the Pantheon, top notch museums collectively with the Louvre and Musee d'Orsay, the cutest cafés which incorporates Laduree, present day avenues together with the Champs Elysees, and challenge parks collectively with Disneyland, you can not deny its attractive enchantment in any state of affairs.

2. France Is A Cultural And Historical Heaven

France is 1000 times extra appealing because of its rich lifestyle and information. The French are very happy with their historical beyond. The essential battles of the French Revolution and Napoleonic duration are honored thru art work, shape, and literature. In France, you may despite the fact that see time being preserved thru points of interest which include the Palace of Versailles, Notre Dame Cathedral, Sacre-Coeur, Old Port of Marseille, and others. France has almost 39 monuments on the UNESCO World Heritage Site listing, highlighting its massive cultural importance sooner or later of human statistics.

3. French cuisine is a culinary treasure.

French cuisine is an important problem of the culinary international. It preserves France's popularity no longer only for its remarkable and rich flavor however moreover for its precious recipes and cooking competencies, which can be critical gastronomical treasures. Every foodie ought to attempt real, conventional, and nearby French delicacies. Your gastronomic adventure is probably otherworldly, with croissants, baguettes, shellfish, and over four hundred forms of cheese to select from.

4. Fashion Lovers' Paradise

Famous fashion houses in France embody Dior, Chanel, and Louis Vuitton. For the fashionista in you, France is a clients' paradise. You may go along the renowned streets and save till you drop. Not only that, but the complete French network will function concept for your material cupboard refresh. Even on a ordinary day, people in France want to reveal off their high priced fashion enjoy as they walk down the street. Many fashion labels may even host Fashion Week activities wherein you can have a study the contemporary-day series and possibly buy a number of the most visually attractive objects of apparel. Some of the fine streets for dressing up embody Rue de Rivoli, Champs Elysees, and Les Halles.

five. Geographically Diverse Country

With its particular panorama, France offers more possibilities for tourists. If you need to swim, surf, snorkel, or clearly lighten up on a seaside within the solar? Go immediately to Cannes, Nice, or the Cote d'Azur. Do you need to spend your tour skiing on your coronary coronary coronary heart's pride on the snowy slopes? They go to Mont Blanc. France offers a place for every organization assignment.

6. Land of Art and Museum

We're pretty advantageous you are aware that France is a place of artwork and museums. Every place of France has a museum on the manner to amaze you with famous masterpieces, from the Louvre Museum (the World's Largest Museum) that holds massive artistic endeavors like Leonardo da Vinci's painting of the Mona Lisa to the incredible series of modern-day artwork at Centre Pompidou.

7. Wine Enthusiast Vacation

If you're a wine aficionado who desires to sample the arena's great wines, there can be no better location to visit than France. In France, there are round 450 notable varieties of handmade wine collections to pick from. Every vicinity has its vicinity of facts, and also you may not be able to withstand eating all of the responsibility-unfastened wines without turning into bored.

eight. Enchanting castles

There are numerous castles in France. You may spend a whole month exploring all of the castles of Gothic and Romanesque form. The outstanding trouble is that you may stay in a number of them and marvel at their beauty. From the Chateau de Chantilly to the Palace of Versailles and the Château de Chenonceau, the ones splendid castles will take your breath away and provide you with a modern day perspective on France.

nine. Countryside Relaxation

If you want to get away from the hustle and bustle of the city, there may be no better spot than France's lovely geographical location. To be easy, villages make up extra than 80% of France. They provide a giant diploma of calm and quiet that lets in you to miss approximately your problems and spend time with the locals, cherishing every minute through imprinting the terrifi surroundings in your reminiscence.

10. Romance Hotspot

Finally, the most crucial motive to place France for your bucket list is that France makes it difficult to disregard its romantic thing. The refinement of the French language contributes to amorous endeavors within the "city of affection."

The Top 15 Things to Do and See in France

1. Spend a while in Paris.

The Louvre, impressionist museums, the Eiffel Tower, the Seine, wonderful parks, jazz, and first-rate cuisine abound in Paris. It is as outstanding as people declare, and even though seeing all of it might take a life-time, 4 or five days can offer you with a first rate have an effect on. It's taken into consideration certainly one of my all-time preferred towns.

2. Visit the Loire Valley

The Loire is adorable, with many vineyards and chateaux. The place is domestic to some of the area's excellent wines, in addition to fascinating tiny villages and delicious cuisine. It's a want to-see region. It is my favorite place in France.

3. Tour Marseille

Marseille is a metropolitan metropolis with a wealthy information, remarkable restaurants, theaters, museums, or maybe an international soccer stadium. While the town is tough and commercial, it is worth a go to for its lovable waterfront and various cultural combination.

four. Spend time in Nice

Nice is pleasant (does it make revel in?). This seaside hamlet in the south is well-known with fee range travelers who want to take in some solar however can't come up with the money for Cannes or Monaco. I don't accept as true with the seashore right right here is superb, however its vital characteristic permits you to with out problem go to the remainder of the coast (and it's miles nicer beaches).

five. Drink wine in Bordeaux

Bordeaux produces some of the arena's quality wines. While it's far an costly vicinity, it's miles amazing and well truely really worth the cash. Bordeaux gives Europe's longest retail strip, delicious seafood (try Le Petit Commerce), a ancient center, and, of path, wine. It's my favored location in France, 2d simplest to Paris.

6. Discover Lyon's facts

Lyon is surrounded by using the use of beautiful castles and tiny towns. It's best for those who need to appearance the French geographical vicinity and move lower back in time to medieval France. The complete metropolis is a UNESCO World Heritage net page, and it looks like you've got lengthy past lower back in time. Visit the botanical garden, the basilica, and the city's Old Quarter.

7. Mingle with the rich in Monaco

Monaco is a French Riviera independent town-kingdom. Winding avenues, suitable houses, a international-famous online casino, and huge contemporary boats may also additionally moreover all be found on this little country. Spend time with the properly-to-do who throng to the Cote d'Azur from all round France throughout the summer time. It is one of the international's tiniest international places, spanning just a few square kilometers and domestic to plenty less than forty,000 people.

8. Go to Alsace.

This northeast location near the German border is a lovable spot to discover. The area is characterized with the resource of a mixture of Germanic and French impacts, and the number one attraction is the ancient town of Colmar. Some of the systems on the town date again to the 1300s, making it the most appealing French metropolis viable!

9. Take a walk in Parc de la Villette.

This Parisian park is domestic to a systematic museum in addition to extremely good unusual sights. There are numerous architectural follies, challenge gardens, and open locations for sports and discovery. It changed into created for every youngsters and adults and is a amusing place to visit.

10. Go once more to the trenches

France emerge as the epicenter of World War I (1914-1918), and there are nevertheless numerous reminders of the devastation that became wrecked in the course of the ones years anywhere within the state. Two great fights, for example, passed off at Vimy Ridge (which became a amazing victory for Canadian soldiers) and Verdun. Both locations feature terrific traveler centers and traveler services. It's a touching and enlightening revel in.

11. Explore Roman ruins

Outside of Italy, France possesses some of the best Roman stays. Orange, Nimes, and Arles all have lovely Roman theaters, and Nimes moreover has a well-preserved temple (I favored Nimes). It's unexpected to find out so many relics of Roman authority within the south of France, and these places are well really worth a go to.

12. Go snowboarding

The French Alps include a number of Europe's top ski slopes. If you're in Europe sooner or later of the winter and do not know what to do, strive organizing a collection and renting a ski lodge, or staying at one of the slope-facet lodges or hostels. Bring hundreds of beer and wine to maintain you toasty after an afternoon at the hills. It need to be stated that skiing in France isn't always cheap (existence passes might cost a touch as an awful lot as seventy five EUR steady with day).

thirteen. See additionally Dune de Pyla.

This dune is positioned in Pyla Sur Mer, a vacation city wherein lots of France's nicely-to-do spend the summer season. It is Europe's largest dune, fashioned with the useful resource of winds eroding one edge of the bay and throwing sand throughout. The dune is over three kilometers (2 miles) lengthy and might reap heights of one hundred ten meters (360 feet) in certain spots.

14. Visit the Louvre

The Louvre is the world's biggest museum, overlaying masses of square feet and housing loads and masses of artifacts and pieces of art (which encompass the Mona Lisa and the Venus de Milo). To see the entirety, you can need at the least two entire days, notwithstanding the fact that you may see the highlights in simplest in some unspecified time in the future. It costs €17.

15. Go diving

Although diving might not be the primary element that springs to thoughts on the same time as you think about France, Marseille is brief becoming america's diving capital. Travel to the Mediterranean to find out tunnels and caverns and respect cute marine sponges, anemones, and sea enthusiasts. There also are moray eels and octopus to be determined, further to numerous shipwrecks together with the Le Liban (1882) and the Le Chaouen (1961). The amazing months for diving right proper here are from June via October even as the water is particularly warmer. Prices begin at 100 EUR.

8 do's and don'ts of France

France is the land of crispy baguettes, delectable pastries, and remarkable wine. Because France is all about taking part within the higher things in lifestyles, it is no surprise that a number of the cultural do's and don'ts revolve round delicacies. Read on for a few suggestions and conventions to guarantee you in form in without problems and are a achievement at Parisian sosoirées.

1.SERVICE SAVOIR-FAIRE

You should not top off your glass. Wait to be served alternatively. If you have been looking longingly at the wine bottle at the table for half of-hour, ask your neighbor inside the event that that they'd need a top off. If they solution positive, it is a win-win scenario: you can first serve your neighbor and then pour a few for yourself. Top tip: When pouring, endure in thoughts no longer to fill the glass to the pinnacle - restraint is critical for the French.

When tipping, round as a whole lot as the subsequent huge range. While the company charge is blanketed, customers commonly do not need their unique exchange decrease lower back. And, if the company end up notable (a totally real opportunity, opposite to famous belief), you can usually tip extra.

2. BREAD BREAKING

Buy baguettes instead of one. Baguette is a commonplace French cuisine. Baguette with salted butter and jam for breakfast. Lunch? Salad on a baguette. Dinner? A heat cream soup. Served with baguette. So, if you're heading to the bakery to get a freshly made baguette, why no longer get ?

Do not use a knife to reduce the baguette. Don't even keep in mind cleanly lowering the baguette. Place it on a awesome fabric or in its authentic paper wrapping on the table and allow all of us rip a chunk off it as they desire.

3. ETIQUETTE SUCCESS

Maintain every fingers on the desk. While it is everyday in high-quality worldwide locations to keep one's hand on one's lap, the French will scoff. Always keep your palms visible, however hold your elbows included - in no way rest them at the desk.

Make no slurping sounds. It's considered terrible etiquette to lap up your soup with exuberant sounds, regardless of how hundreds you like your bouillabaisse or soupe à l'oignon.

four.WIELDING A KNIFE

You want to not chop your salad. Instead of lowering your mixed vegetables, fold them into small bundles alongside facet your utensils. Voilà!

Use a particular knife to chop the cheese. Each type of cheese has its knife: difficult cheeses want a tear-common knife, even as moderate cheeses name for a mild, blunt region. To make topics even extra tough, every cheese have to be chopped in a effective manner - but we're going to reserve that for some other blog article.

5. BEING CASUALLY CHIC

Leave the wearing device at home. Basketball shorts and jerseys are only authorized to be worn on the court docket and no longer on the street. Pajamas are also off-limits; no going to the shop to your velvet pajamas and hoping no character notices. They actually will.

Don't pass overboard, each. We all are aware of it's a touchy line. The purpose is to take some time however no longer overdo it; picture untidy hair and lipstick or easy tennis shoes with a smart outfit.

6. ART OF THE 'BISE'

Avoid being uncomfortable. If you're aware of courteous handshakes or uncomfortable pats on the back, bise-ing may additionally seem bizarre. Dive in and air kiss your friend on every cheeks, softly pouting and developing a kissing sound. To add to the intrigue, the amount of kisses varies consistent with locale.

Everyone need to be greeted in my view. When you be a part of up with a set of friends, make the effort to welcome everyone in my view or together. There can be no selective bise-ing! When you leave, repeat the everyday; no slipping out; your friends will word and hold it towards you.

7. KEEPING IT COOL

For someone you do no longer realize, use 'vous'. When dubious, typically use the formal 'vous' shape. It will prevent you from uncomfortable glances and merciless solutions. It is not uncommon to concentrate human beings fluidly float from 'vous' to 'tu' within the middle of a speak as they get higher familiar with every special.

Don't be too emotional. Even if you need to scream with delight, it is crucial to be modest and blasé in France. Work in your poker face and mild shoulder shrug. Share your pleasures and disappointments, however do now not turn your target market off through manner of being too open.

8. SANTÉ!

Don't begin ingesting until everybody has been served. Drinking, like consuming, has its traditions at a French table. Before you're taking your first flavor, make certain clearly each person's cups are whole and all people has cheered. Sharing a meal is a social occasion; do now not do it by myself!

Drink gently. The French do no longer consume to meet hunger or drink to alleviate thirst; as an opportunity, they nibble on their food and take little sips. Don't slurp your wine; the factor is to revel in the dinner and make communique!

Chapter 11: Tourist Attractions In France

According to facts accumulated by the United Nations World Tourism Organization, France ranks first in the global in terms of tourism, attracting 80 a million global tourists every 365 days. Cities with robust cultural significance, together with Paris, Toulouse, Lyon, and Bordeaux, have 37 international history web sites in universal. France is likewise diagnosed for its lovable seashores, castles, ancient museums, and beautiful gardens and parks. The following are the most famous visitor websites in France.

1. Paris' Eiffel Tower

One of Paris' maximum identified landmarks. It emerge as constructed in 1889 as an the the front arc to the Universal Exposition or World's Fair. It can be the very great guy-made constructing inside the worldwide for the subsequent forty one years, reputation at 320 meters. The Eiffel Tower's introduction commenced in 1887 and took years to finish. It have become named after Gustave Eiffel, the French architect in price of the Eiffel Tower's construction.

The Eiffel Tower is built with spherical 10,000 tonnes of iron. As the Eiffel Tower have come to be an the world over well-known constructing, it became rebuilt in Nevada, the United States, and Tokyo. The tower want to be repainted every seven years to save you corrosion, which calls for 50 tonnes of paint. Tourists might also additionally go to the number one flooring of the Eiffel Tower via the use of stairway or lifestyles.

2. Disneyland, Paris

In 1992, the Disneyland leisure complex opened in downtown Paris. As of 2014, it's been visited over 275 million instances through the use of the usage of vacationers, making it considered one in every of Paris's maximum popular internet websites. Disneyland spans 4800 acres and includes subject matter parks, hotels, retail, and leisure regions.

There are 57 rides, sixty two shops, 5800 motel rooms, and 55463 employees divided among 500 divisions. The Pirates of the Caribbean experience is the most popular, with 6.7 million traffic in 2011. It is based totally at the very famous Hollywood film Pirates of the Caribbean, which starred Johnny Depp.

The little global, vicinity mountain: Mission 2, Big Thunder Mountain, and Buzz Lightyear laser blast are all protected in this episode. The Walt Disney Studios Park, which opened in 2002, protected film-themed points of hobby, inside the decrease back of-the-scenes film era, and film-themed corporations. The Disney Village offers web page visitors with a whole lot of leisure venues, eateries, and buying possibilities. The Walt Disney Studios inner Disneyland Paris display movie-themed factors of hobby, within the back of-the-scenes pix from blockbuster movies, and display industrial business enterprise.

three. Palace Versailles, Ile de France Region

The Palace of Versailles, generally referred to as Château de Versailles, is France's grandest palace. The earliest part of this mansion changed into erected as a searching resort with the aid of King Louis XIII in 1624. Later, Louis XIV, the successor of Louis XIII, prolonged it to become the u . S .'s largest palace. The palace has seven-hundred rooms, 2153 domestic home windows, 68 staircases, and a beautiful park of 2000 acres.

Nowadays, the Palace of Versailles is the us's maximum well-known visitor vacation spot. It also serves as a venue for some of political capabilities. The chambers inside the palace range in size and decor depending at the recognition of the person that lives there.

The hall of mirrors, which diffuses the daytime, becomes the maximum sizeable area of the palace for traffic to visit. The lawn of the Palace of Versailles grow to be designed inside the French fashion and comprised 200000 timber, greater than million plants of severa sorts, and 50 lovely fountains.

4. Louvre, Paris

One of the world's biggest museums, placed in Paris. This museum's first-rate paintings collection makes it the most visited museum within the global. 35000 prehistoric artifacts are on show, which encompass Egyptian treasures, royal jewels, historical artwork, and historical sculptures.

The museum is a section of Louvre mansion, a medieval-era baroque-style mansion. The Louvre Museum on the start opened its doors in 1763. Later, Emperor Napoleon contributed a big quantity of portions of artwork to the museum. French rulers furthermore contributed to the museum's series of ancient artifacts.

This museum has eight primary divisions wherein the gadgets are displayed. The eight primary departments of the Louvre Museum encompass Eastern antiquities, Egyptian antiquities, Greek, Etruscan, Roman antiquities, Islamic arts, sculptures, decorative arts, art work, prints, and drawings, with artifacts starting from the sixth century BC to the nineteenth century AD. Another awesome feature of this museum is the Louvre pyramid, which emerge as created through I.M Pei.

five. Saint Michel,Normandy

It is one in every of Europe's maximum iconic factors of interest and a renowned spiritual destination, located on the island of Normandy. The abbey that encompasses about 1 km in circumference is the island's most famous characteristic. The abbey, church, and monastery are placed in the pinnacle a part of Saint Michel. The backside thing has shops, halls, and homes. This landmark, every other World Heritage landmark of France, has over 3 million vacationers each one year.

Pilgrims can also effects technique the monastery thinking about Saint Michel is really 6000 meters distant from the land. Visitors might also get right of get right of entry to to the top galley at the roof of the monastery by using the famous lace staircase, which requires 900 steps to reap the top of the abbey. A specific exhibition at the Saint Michel Museum teaches traffic approximately the facts and constructing of this extremely good shape.

6. Château De Chambord, Loir et Cher

The biggest unfinished château in the Loire Valley is placed in important France. It is the exceptional instance of French Renaissance form in the international. Surprisingly, the complete manor domestic is encircled with the aid of manner of the state's largest wooded location park. It turned into designed as a searching inn for King Francois I. It is now in reality one among France's maximum distinguished tourist locations and a UNESCO World Heritage Site.

Starting introduction in 1519, it took 28 years to gain its current united states. However, the château have grow to be by no means completed in the aftermath of the French Revolution. The inner detail of the chateau suggests French and Italian aptitude inside the arranging of rooms and suites.

This château has 440 rooms, 80 staircases, and 280 fireplaces. It additionally has a whole lot of towers and chimneys. The guided excursion of the citadel allows tourists to view all of the key areas of the chateau and find out approximately the building strategies and architectural styles.

7. Verdon Gorge Canyon , Alpes de Haute Provence

It is also called the "Grand Canyon of Europe," and it is placed inside the region of Alpes De Haute in Southeastern France. This river canyon is spherical 25 kilometers long and has seven hundred-meter-immoderate partitions. It is famous for the turquoise-green hue of the Verdon River internal that location, it sincerely is due to minerals from rock and glacial sources.

The rims of this river canyon provide excellent perspectives of the encompassing regions, attracting a large sort of site visitors. Kayaking at the green-coloured water of the Verdon River is also a memorable experience for website site visitors. Hiking, canoeing, paragliding, rafting, and hiking are a number of the more sports available within the Verdon Gorge Canyon.

eight. Paris, Arc De Triomphe

The Arc de Triomphe is the maximum famous triumphal arch in Paris. In 1806 French Emperor Napoleon ordered the erection of this monument to commemorate the heroes who fought beside him in some of conflicts. It changed into opened in 1836 after creation changed into halted typically after Emperor Napoleon's abdication.

The historical astylar style emerge as completed to construct this monument. On the white outside of this monument, the names of all conflicts of the First French Republic and Napoleonic conflicts are also inscribed. Under the vault of this monument is placed the tomb of an unknown soldier from World War I.

nine. Pont Du Gard Bridge,Nime

It is a large Ancient Roman bridge that spans the Gardon River in Rome, Southern France. The bridge is 50 kilometers extended and modified into erected within the first century AD. It changed into used by the historic Romans to move water from France's Uzes commune to Nime. It is also one of the UNESCO World Heritage Sites.

This bridge end up built the usage of yellow limestones, breeze blocks, and calcium deposits. The Pont Du Gard bridge has 3-tier arches and is forty eight.Eight meters tall. Until the sixth century, the Romans sent 200000 cubic meters of water every day to Nimes, and it emerge as in a while carried out as a toll bridge.

10. Paris' Basilica of the Sacred Heart

One of Paris' maximum iconic monuments, a Roman Catholic church perched on

Montmartre Hill, the town's maximum factor. This basilica is devoted to Jesus' valuable coronary coronary heart. It have become created thru French architect Paul Abadie and constructed between 1875 and 1914.

This cathedral changed into built of Travertine stones, a kind of limestone created by using manner of way of the interest of warm springs. It slowly and progressively releases calcite, permitting it to live white even under severe weather conditions. A spacious meditation corridor with a fountain changed into constructed on this church. Tourists can also experience a lovely panoramic view of Paris from the top of the dome of the Basilica of the Sacred Heart.

Chapter 12: Ideal France Five-Days Itineraries

To make the maximum of a five-day holiday to France, cope with one area. While it may be tempting to find out greater land, maintaining to at the least one geographical area saves time and can pleasantly surprise you with how awesome the perspectives and sports activities may be even within a short distance. Bordeaux, for example, is famed for its tremendous wines, however it furthermore has seashores and motorcycle rides. A avenue energy throughout Provence might also moreover take you beyond cities, vineyards, and the vintage-meets-new hustle and bustle of metropolitan Marseille.

Itinerary 1: A French Riviera Gateway

This speedy-paced avenue experience is not approximately thrilling at the seaside (although there may be time for that as well), but as an opportunity approximately checking off severa must-see places in France's sunny southeast place for people who pick out out to be at the circulate.

Spend your first night time time near the Italian border at Menton.

Pick up your apartment vehicle in Nice and strength to Eze, a medieval hamlet constructed on a totally immoderate cliff with art work galleries and breathtaking perspectives of the coast, in particular from the Jardin Exotique d'eze, a cactus lawn on the pinnacle of the municipality. Then, save you at Roquebrune-Cap-Martin to look some ancient castles in advance than persevering with to beachfront Menton in time for a Mediterranean sunset.

Following which may be a series of hilltop businesses like Gourdon, Saint Paul de Vence, and Grasse, wherein you may get hundreds of workout through wandering across the twisting streets and neighboring hillsides. Then flow again to the coast and forestall at Port Grimaud, called "Venice of Provence," for supper, which has small boutiques and remarkable consuming places. You'll have time to explore the Massif des Maures, a huge mountain vicinity with several hiking and bike paths. Alternatively, you will likely go to Collobrières, France's chestnut center, to get nearby substances and delectable presents.

The tour returns to Nice, in which you may have time to find out the beaches and most important points of interest which incorporates the Promenade des Anglais, the Chagall Museum, and the Museum of Modern and Contemporary Art. Spend your very last night time time consuming top notch seafood and taking within the town's colourful road scene. Find out more

Itinerary 2: Bordeaux for Wine Lovers

Oenophiles can also additionally discover this itinerary focused on the famed Bordeaux wine-growing region. The pedestrian-pleasant metropolis of the equal name serves as your own home base for the entire journey, and it is one of France's most exciting, amazing, and dynamic towns.

Attend winery tours and tastings at a number of Bordeaux's best wineries.

Furthermore, at the least half of of of the town is UNESCO-listed, making it the area's biggest metropolis international historical past net net web page. You'll have masses of time to discover Bordeaux's chic coffee stores, meals trucks, eating places, and wine bars for your private.

You'll moreover pass on a private tour of Bordeaux's Capucin Farmer's Market, wherein you could discover about the riverside port's significance within the wine change from the Middle Ages to the present. A manual can also moreover even take you on the city's sleek, current tram to the Le Musée du Vin et du Négoce, a wine museum set in an 18th-century wine cellar.

The following four days might be spent journeying Bordeaux's surroundings, starting with a bicycle ride through the vineyards of Saint Emilion, that permits you to encompass tours and tastings at beautiful châteaux. You'll furthermore see Arcachon's Bay on the Atlantic Coast, climb Pyla's Sand Dune (Europe's largest dune), and pattern easy oysters from a close-by grower. The adventure concludes with a stress along the Medoc's 'Château Route,' wherein you may go to a Great Classified Growth belongings—certainly one of Bordeaux's maximum distinguished chateaux. This is in which you can get a whole clarification in their winemaking way, in addition to a risk to pattern the estate's legendary pours. Find out extra

Itinerary three: Excursion to the Normandy Coast

This itinerary targeted on Normandy, a region in northern France with an extraordinary chronology spanning the preceding 9 centuries, is certain to enchantment to records aficionados.

Your journey starts offevolved in Paris, wherein you'll have a guided half of-day excursion of the city's factors of interest in advance than boarding a train to Bayeux, your property base for the journey. This charming town is teeming with incredible 13th- to 18th-century structures, together with a brilliant Gothic cathedral and high-quality eateries, which you may discover at your entertainment. You need to moreover see the Bayeux Tapestry, a 229-foot-prolonged (70-meter-prolonged) embroidered linen representing events principal as lots as the Norman invasion of England. You'll additionally have time to explore greater William the Conqueror-related web sites.

A few days of this journey are committed to viewing a number of Normandy's brilliant WWII landmarks, starting with the D-Day touchdown beaches and the courageous warriors who battled for freedom in 1944. This skills Pointe du Hoc, a lovable top scarred via manner of aviation and naval bombardment, in addition to Normandy's coastal battleground websites, which encompass Omaha Beach, one of landing locations in which thousands of Americans died. In Colleville, you could additionally see a German cemetery and an American cemetery with 9,387 graves spread over a hundred and seventy acres. In addition, your guide will take you to the Mémorial de Caen, a museum and army monument with approximately 90 acres of gardens.

Finish the experience with a complete-day tour of Mont Saint Michel, considered actually one among France's maximum well-known vacationer locations. This beautiful island, topped with a gravity-defying medieval monastery, offers a amazing vista that is well nicely worth the variety of stairs required to get there. If you are fortunate, you can even meet one of the priests and concentrate their Gregorian Chants resonating at some stage in the church in the course of mass. Your manual might also even take you into the village's small cobblestone alleyways, in which you may upward push up and personal with the granite or half of of of-timbered homes.

Itinerary 4: Château Tour within the Loire Valley

The Loire Valley is the spotlight of this itinerary, a rich location south of Paris packed with loads of high-priced châteaux (and their gardens) that previously belonged to kings, queens, dukes, and famous artists.

Upon arrival via rail, you may first go to Château Villandry, the Loire Valley's ultimate Renaissance-era citadel. The subsequent prevent is Château d'Azay le Rideau, that have end up erected on an island in the 16th century underneath the patronage of King Francis the first, with a complex mixture of French ancient past and progressive Italian décor. If time allows, your manual can even take you via Tours, wherein you may pattern some of France's best subculture and food earlier than going to Amboise, your property base for exploring the Loire Valley.

You'll see numerous exceptional chateaux over the following few days, which encompass Château de Chambord, which has four hundred+ rooms and a stunning double spiral staircase most important to the royal suites of François I and Louis XIV. There's additionally Château de Chenonceau, a -tale gallery that stands above the Loire River and is one of the most famend landmarks within the Loire Valley. Then there can be Chaumont sur Loire, with stables that had been considered the most high-priced in Europe towards the end of the nineteenth century.

But it is not superb about traveling round to various chateaux: There may be time for additonal sports, which includes wine tasting in an eleventh-century troglodyte cellar that changed into formerly a quarry. You may additionally moreover find out Amboise on foot or on an e-bike to see Leonardo da Vinci's awesome residence from greater than 500 years within the beyond. While you are right right here, take a stroll throughout the cute green park and see wherein the artist had amazing banquets for his high-priced pal, King Francis 1st. Find out more

Itinerary 5: The Perfect Provençal Road Trip

Perhaps no different place higher captures France's particular splendor than Provence. Make the maximum of it slow with this self-force itinerary that takes you to a new in a single day location each night time time time, starting with France's oldest metropolis, Marseille.

Park your car in Marseille and walk thru the metropolis's 2000-one year data, which consist of distinguished regions like Le Panier. As the sun gadgets, make your way to the Vieux-Port and get a pastis (anise-flavored apéritif).

Then journey to Aix en Provence, a medieval town surrounded with the aid of using Provençal cities and environment famed for vineyards, lavender-protected fields, and limestone cliffs—iconic vistas immortalized in the works of artists together with Cezanne and Picasso. Then, discover Les Baux de Provence, which dates again to six,000 BCE and is appeared as certainly taken into consideration certainly one of France's maximum picturesque towns. Stroll round this nicely-preserved metropolis, preventing via manner of historical church homes and the Château des Baux de Provence, a fortified castle constructed within the 10th century. An top notch multimedia artwork display is also provided in a disused quarry near the citadel in advance than taking location to neighboring Saint Remy de Provence.

From proper right here, you may discover a number of the pinnacle Rhône Valley vineyards, along side Châteauneuf du Pape. The remains of the Pope's high-quality summer time palace dominate this conventional medieval hamlet, in which no tons much less than thirteen grape sorts mixture with the numerous soils to offer a giant sort of complex crimson wines and sensitive white wines. This wine-themed day concludes certainly in Avignon, in which you can sample the town's various eating scene, which incorporates the whole lot from informal bistros to Michelin-starred tasting menus.

Chapter 13: Obtaining France Tourist Visa

Documents Required for a France Schengen Visa

Completed or translated files for a French Schengen visa software program program have to be in English, French, or Spanish.

A valid passport is needed.

A minimum of blank pages

With the applicant's signature Not older than ten years

Valid for at the least 3 months after the preferred visa expires.

Previous passport, if important

Photos the dimensions of a passport

3.5 x four.Five cm in duration

A easy white backdrop

Within the ultimate six months

looking forward to stand trends great and exquisite

software shape finished

Fingerprint biometric facts

Fee for France Schengen Visa

Documents associated with your adventure

Travel Itinerary or technique

Proof of move again to domestic or forwarding charge price tag to some different united states of the united states

Reason for journeying France

Reservations for flights

Proof of monetary technique (financial institution statements from the previous 3 months, personal property, and/or different assets)

Proof of hotels (collectively with booking reference variety, area, and hotel touch variety)

Travel scientific medical health insurance

Valid in a few unspecified time in the future of the visa.

All Schengen international places are protected.

A minimal of 30,000 EUR in insurance want to be acquired.

The validity, period, and scope of your insurance want to be unique on the confirmation letter or insurance office artwork.

Letter of employment with the following information:

Employer's call and cope with

The nature of the hobby

The begin date of employment

Salary

The reason for the experience

Time have come to be taken off from paintings for journey

scans (copies):

Personal ID web page of passport .

Older Schengen visas (wherein applicable).

Permit to are living (if relevant).

Applicants under the age of 18 ought to gift the subsequent extra documentation:

Birth certificates reproduction

Adoption papers are crucial if the minor applicant is observed.

Divorce papers are important if the underage applicant's parents are divorced.

Death certificates are crucial if the underage applicant's parents are useless.

Consent letter from each dad and mom or legal guardians

Copies of every mother and father or legal guardians' passports

Supplementary documentation additionally can be required in connection with your adventure visa software program program.

France Schengen Visa Fees

The standard software price for a French Schengen visa is 80 EUR. However, some applicants are free from prices, including maximum student visas and visas for youngsters underneath the age of six. Applicants want to encompass a non-refundable organization fee with their software.

France Application Procedures

Prepare all the essential documentation.

On the visa software program shape, pick "Tourism" due to the fact the motive for journey.

Determine the huge kind of entries required to go into France or the Schengen location.

Complete the utility form.

In most times, packages for a French Schengen visa are submitted on line using the u . S . A .'s application internet site on line. It is available in Arabic, Chinese, Russian, and Spanish, further to English and French.

Register in case you are a modern-day individual, or log in in case you are an present person.

Fill out the software form and post it, then print it in conjunction with the receipt.

This paper application replica, together with any supplementary papers relevant on your utility, want to be introduced to a French Consulate or visa processing facility.

Make a visa appointment, if essential.

The majority of applications need an in-person appointment at the closest French Consulate or visa facility to be submitted. Alternatively, applications may be submitted for the duration of ordinary organisation hours with out an appointment. To find out whether or now not or not an appointment is wanted, touch the French Consulate or a visa facility.

Submit your software for a French Schengen visa.

Please preserve in thoughts that packages have to be filed at the least 15 days earlier than the date of excursion however no sooner than 6 months in advance.

In most instances, programs have to be furnished in man or woman to a French Consulate or a visa processing place of work. The submission strategies, but, can also moreover trade highly.

Applicants will very absolutely be requested to provide their fingerprints (biometric information). Children underneath the age of 12 are excused from having their fingerprints taken. Applicants who have already furnished their fingerprints within the past 59 months aren't probably to be requested to acquire this another time.

You should pay the visa utility rate.

banner

When to Apply

Visa packages need to be filed at least 15 days earlier than departure, however no in advance than 6 months in advance than departure.

Where Can I Apply for a Visa in France?

Visa applications want to be sent to a French consulate or a visa software program facility affiliated with France.

Only programs inside the u . S . A . Of citizenship or residency have to be filed.

Applications may be made via a Schengen united states of america consulate representing the pursuits of a French consulate in international places wherein there may be no French consulate.

VIsa Processing Time in France

French Schengen visa packages are normally processed in 15 to 60 days.

For ordinary visa packages, applicants want to make sure that the information on the visa is accurate and updated even as it is amassed.

Applicants who have were given their Schengen Visa for France want to hold the following records in thoughts:

After your submission is entire, notify the French Consulate or visa utility center of any modifications for your time desk.

The issuance of a Schengen visa does no longer make sure get proper of get entry to to to France or incredible Schengen nations.

Additional documentation regarding your economic scenario or housing also can nonetheless be desired for front into France or other Schengen worldwide locations.

In the case of refused visa programs:

If your software program for a French Schengen visa modified into denied, you have months to attraction the choice.

Applicants will be given a elegant-issued French Schengen visa rejection file outlining the appeal manner and the motive for the visa software application's denial.

The Schengen visa enchantment need to be submitted in writing and signed in French.

The petition want to be filed with the Commission de Recours Contre les Décisions de Refus de Visa.

Depending at the reason of the visa refusal, candidates might also furthermore possibly document an appeal with the French administrative courtroom docket.

For the attraction to be processed, a non-refundable appeal fee can be required.

Chapter 14: France Travel Cost

Dorm rooms at hostels with eight-10 beds cost among 20 and forty EUR consistent with night time, with Paris being the most expensive. Private rooms at hostels might cost a touch as a lot as 75 EUR normal with night time time time. Free Wi-Fi is regular, and a few hostels offer self-catering alternatives.

A double room with unfastened WiFi and air con starts offevolved at kind of 60 EUR regular with night time time time in a price variety inn. Outside of Paris, Bordeaux, and the French Riviera, resorts is much less steeply-priced.

Airbnb is obtainable throughout the united states. Private rooms start at form of 35 EUR, while entire houses/apartments begin at sixty 5 EUR (despite the fact that normally value at the least instances that a bargain, particularly in Paris).

Camping is offered at some stage in the kingdom for every person going with a tent. A easy net web page with out electricity for 2 people prices extra or much less 22 EUR in line with night time time. In France, wild tenting is against the law.

Food - Food has an extended records in France and is deeply connected to manner of existence. Fresh bread (specifically baguettes), proper network cheeses, and sufficient wine can be traditional culinary mainstays, but they're some of the us's need to-consume delicacies. Try the croque monsieur (a heat ham and cheese sandwich), pot-au-feu (red meat stew), steak frites (steak and fries), and in case you're feeling very bold, frog legs, escargot (snails), or foie gras (a fattened duck or goose liver).

Buying your meals in France may be pretty less costly and is the greatest way to sample the delicacies of the kingdom. There are numerous bread, cheese, and meat stores nearby, and this is how the French consume. They visit their community marketplaces, wherein they buy food and put together it.

You can prepare dinner dinner your lunch for two people for form of ten euros (with wine in case you're current-day enough). Sandwiches at much less costly community stores fee about four-7 EUR.

In contrast, a supper at a eating place prices between 20 and 35 EUR, collectively with a pitcher of wine.

A combination lunch at a brief meals restaurant (which incorporates McDonald's) charges sort of 9 EUR. An much less costly supper at a informal take-out restaurant will price you form of 10-15 EUR.

Beer fees spherical 6-7 EUR, whilst a cappuccino/latte expenses about three EUR. Bottled water costs one euro.

Expect to spend 45-sixty five EUR on groceries for in step with week in case you intend on making ready your food. This includes vital necessities which includes bread, pasta, seasonal fruit, and meat.

Most points of interest and museum admission expenses range among 10 and 20 EUR. A half of-day wine tour fees form of 70-ninety EUR. The fee of trekking the Eiffel Tower is among 16 and 26 EUR. The Versailles Palace and Gardens price 27 EUR to appearance. The Louvre is 17 EUR, at the same time as diving is round one hundred EUR.

Traveling on a Budget in France

Prepare to spend 70 EUR an afternoon on a backpacker's rate range. On this budget, you may stay in hostel dormitories, prepare all your food, use public transit, restriction your eating, and keep on with in the essential unfastened and plenty less high priced sports activities sports like loose strolling tours, parks and gardens, and unfastened museums.

On a each day price range of 155 EUR, you could live in a non-public Airbnb, dine out for most meals, have a few drinks, tour the teach among towns, and participate in extra paid activities together with wine excursions and a go to to Versailles.

A "costly" budget of 300 EUR or greater constant with day lets in you to live in lodges, dine out for all meals, lease a vehicle to head approximately, drink greater, and participate in any excursions and sports activities you choice. However, this is sincerely the number one stage of high-priced. The most effective limit is your imagination!

Ways to Save Money While Visiting France

If you are not cautious, France might in all likelihood smash your finances. Fortunately, there are different strategies to shop here as well. Here are a few cash-saving thoughts to get you started:

Take a picnic - Eating out in France, mainly in Paris, is an luxurious enjoy. Restaurants may also with out problem deplete a day's coins. Fortunately, not anything says "French" like a picnic. Go to the close by marketplace, get some delicious cheese, bread, fruits, and meats, and experience a picnic on the same time as searching the arena go through. A delicious supper can be had for much less than ten euros.

Take the (slow) train - Train journey in Europe is inexpensive and the maximum convenient approach to move about France. The TGV line isn't cheap, however in case you take the gradual teach or have a Eurail rate tag, you can save money.

Drink wine - In France, wine is honestly as less expensive as water. While you need to now not avoid consuming water, you want to choose wine over other sorts of alcohol to keep coins. A incredible bottle can be had for as low as 3 EUR!

Shop on the markets in case you want to eat terrific French food. Go to the outside markets as the natives do. Visit the cheesemonger, the fishmonger, the bread-monger, and all people else to gather the finest neighborhood additives for a beautiful

French lunch. When in comparison to ingesting out, it saves some of cash.

Prepare in your night day out - Drinking at bars is pretty pricey, specifically in Paris. Drink cheaper wine earlier than going out to hold coins on liquids at pubs.

Avoid clubs - Clubs in France are highly-priced and impose an admission fee (which might also moreover exceed 20 EUR!). Drinks charge as a minimum 12 EUR. Skip the golf equipment if you do no longer want to spend 90 EUR in a single night time.

Ridesharing - If your time desk is flexible, don't forget the ridesharing company BlaBlaCar to percentage rides with locals among cities (or worldwide locations). Drivers are confirmed, and it is honestly steady (however riders do now not continuously show up, this is why you have to be flexible).

Consume a prix-fixe dinner - A prix-fixe meal is a tough and fast lunch menu in which a 2-3 direction meal costs approximately 15-20

EUR. This is a appreciably extra price-powerful desire than ordering from the menu. I continuously eat out for lunch after which prepare supper for myself.

Stay with a native - If you want to store coins on the equal time as learning about the lifestyle, be part of Couchsurfing. This state has a massive quantity of hosts. I advocate utilising the service at the least as fast as to preserve money on inns, meet new friends, analyze close by information, and feature a kitchen to cook dinner in!

Take gain of the fact that you are underneath the age of 26 - France gives EXTENSIVE discounts to oldsters underneath the age of 26.

Make extraordinary to build up an ISIC card if they have one!

Carry a water bottle - Because the faucet water on this area is stable to drink, convey a reusable water bottle to keep cash and reduce your usage of plastic. LifeStraw is my preferred emblem considering that its bottles have incorporated filters that preserve your water natural and secure.

Places to Stay in France

In seek of the first-class hostel in France? Every massive town has a plethora of possibilities. Here are some of my preferred French hostels:

Canal St. Christopher (Paris)

(Paris) Les Piaules

Hostel Generator (Paris)

Gare du Nord St. Christopher (Paris)

Bordeaux Central Hostel

20 Hostel (Bordeaux)

Beach Villa Saint Exupery (Nice)

Vieux-Port Vertigo (Marseille)

How to Travel About in France

The historical harbor changed into crowded with yachts, with the French town of Marseille growing inside the lower again of it.

Local public transportation services are dependable and value about 1-3 EUR for each adventure. The majority of cities and towns have large railroad, bus, and tram networks. Transportation from the airport to the metropolis middle is typically cheaper and accessible.

A "carnet" of ten single-use tickets expenses 14.50 EUR in Paris. A one-day to 5-day pass (a ParisVisite) for all modes of public transportation (bus, metro, trams, and RER suburban trains) expenses amongst thirteen.20 and forty two.20 EUR. It moreover gives reductions on key Parisian landmarks. Tickets may be bought at any metro save you.

To go to Paris from Charles de Gaulle, count on to spend greater or a good deal much less 12 EUR.

Budget Airlines - Budget airlines are outstanding in France, which has numerous large airports. If you are short on time, it's miles an inexpensive and handy choice to excursion during the state.

Paris to Nice costs approximately 50 EUR one manner, and Paris to Marseille expenses shape of the same. To get the exceptional reductions, book at the least a month earlier. These flights can be offered for as low as 15-25 EUR at a few level inside the off-and-shoulder seasons.

Keep in thoughts that most low-price airlines fee extra for checked luggage and occasionally need you to print your price tag beforehand of time.

Buses - There are diverse bus businesses in France, which includes:

Eurolines Flixbus Isilines Ouibus

A 10-hour bus journey from Paris to Marseille fees among 15 and 30 EUR, even as a adventure from Paris to Strasbourg fees among 17 and 25 EUR. A 7.5-hour train experience from Paris to Bordeaux prices round 13 EUR, at the same time as a 3-hour teach adventure from Paris to Tours (within the Loire Valley) charges about 12 EUR. A lengthier journey, which encompass 15 hours from Paris to Nice, fees form of 35 EUR.

While the bus is available, I pick out to pass through rail in France for the reason that it's miles a more terrific and snug enjoy.

Trains - France offers both regular trains and the area-famend immoderate-tempo TGV. The SNCF is France's country wide railway, and tickets can be bought on their internet site. However, journeying the regular educate is notably quicker than taking the bus!

A train rate price tag from Paris to Nice fees among fifty 5 and 100 and 5 EUR if offered very last minute. However, in case you book in advance of time, you may go from Paris to Nice for as low as 25 EUR in 2d elegance. A last-minute educate charge price tag from Paris to Strasbourg expenses 70-80 EUR, despite the fact that advanced second-elegance tickets begin at greater or a good deal much less 19 EUR. Shorter excursions, along side Marseille to Nice, charge kind of 36 EUR, even as Paris to Tours fees 19 EUR. Train tour financial savings are available for passengers under the age of 26!

You might also need to consider looking for a Eurail Pass, which allows passengers to tour Europe by means of the use of manner of giving a super widespread form of stops over a predetermined duration. These passes might be continental, u.S.-precise, or local.

Ridesharing - If your time table is bendy, try a ridesharing provider to seize journeys amongst towns with locals. Drivers are checked, and it's miles completely consistent. It's furthermore generally plenty much less high priced than taking the bus. The maximum well-known is BlaBlaCar. There on occasion a language barrier, but for the most element, it is straightforward to apply and lots more captivating than taking the bus or educate!

Car apartment - France is an super vicinity for a road journey (but keep away from the use of in towns which encompass Paris, which may be a nightmare). A multi-day apartment starts offevolved offevolved at greater or tons much less 30 EUR in line with day. Drivers should be at least 21 years vintage and should have a credit score card of their name.

Hitchhiking is incredibly steady in France, even though it isn't for each person. Make positive you have a sign and are dressed as it have to be. Be flexible as properly, for the reason that wait durations out of doors of massive towns might be prolonged. The best aid for hitchhiking facts is HitchWiki.

Group tour- If you may prefer to see the dominion as part of a set revel in, investigate The Nomadic Network. TNN is a tour commercial employer that I installed for vacationers who want to challenge off the beaten direction and enjoy an area. We offer reasonably-priced small-organization trips to awesome places, bringing humans from anywhere inside the globe together!

Best Time to Visit France

Summer is the height season in France, and it's far pretty busy. Prices upward thrust at some stage in this era, but the general environment and climate are superb, so it is nevertheless worthwhile to return returned sooner or later of pinnacle season. Temperatures variety from 16 to 24 levels Celsius (sixty one to 75 ranges Fahrenheit).

Spring and autumn are shoulder seasons (April-May and September-October, respectively). It's despite the fact that heat, however there aren't as many human beings and the expenses are lower. This is my preferred season to go to France. The weather is great, there are fewer human beings, and the expenses are reduced.

The wintry weather season lasts from November thru February. Even inside the south, it becomes cold. The commonplace winter temperature tiers from zero to 8 ranges Celsius (32 to 46 ranges Fahrenheit). The Christmas season, but, is remarkable - Christmas markets and festivities are abounding!

Staying Safe in France

France is a appreciably strong u . S . For backpacking and solo journey. Because violent crime is uncommon right right here, visitors ought to revel in cushty every day and night time.

However, fraud and minor theft do stand up (particularly in Paris), so hold a be careful. When the usage of crowded public transit, specially in traveler places, generally preserve your valuables stable and out of sight.

Though ordinary precautions practice (in no manner depart your drink on my own at the bar, in no way bypass home by myself drunk, and many others.), solo lady tourists have to experience snug proper here.

One well-known scam in Paris is getting web web page traffic to signal a petition in assist of a shared cause. They'll pester you for a contribution while you sign. To save you being taken gain of, without a doubt refuse all of us who techniques you with a petition.

You also can examine regular journey scams to keep away from right right here to save you extra possible frauds.

In the occasion of an emergency, cellphone 112 for assist.

Always go along with your gut feeling. Make duplicates of your papers, together collectively along with your passport and identity. Send your itinerary to cherished ones in order that they apprehend in which you're.

The most crucial advice I can offer is to have ok journey insurance. Travel insurance will cover you inside the event of contamination, twist of future, robbery, or cancellation. It offers huge insurance if something is going wrong. I in no manner go away the residence without it whilst you consider that I've needed to use it numerous times inside the beyond.

Chapter 15: France Cultural Custom

After we've got addressed the take a look at and living charges in France and completed our articles on studying in France, it is time to talk about French customs and traditions. We wish that this recommendation will assist you in adjusting to French culture and making the most of your academic experience in France.

Language and populace

French is the true language, spoken via as a minimum 88% of the populace, with nearby variations. German dialects are spoken with the resource of spherical 3% of the populace, at the equal time as extraordinary dialects include Breton, Catalan, and Occitan dialects, and languages from former French colonies. As a sophisticated nation, the united states of the us has severa ethnic corporations, which incorporates Basques, Bretons, Africans,

North Africans, Eastern Europeans, Southeast Asians, and others.

France's cultural Traditions

France's way of life changed into inspired by manner of manner of Celtic, Germanic, and Roman elements. It differs from one network and place to the following due to its range. And it is certainly really worth noting that, no matter modern globalization, the dominion has managed to keep tradition in the ones little settlements. And journeying the French countryside is a great possibility to get a taste of the whole thing France has to offer in phrases of manner of lifestyles, customs, and traditions. Don't pass over out on exploring this severa network to your take a look at experience to France!

The significance of French delicacies

French society is particularly worried with its food. Indeed, it's miles one of the cuisines that has obtained exceptional comments from UNESCO. Furthermore, UNESCO placed the

French dinner and its traditions on the list of intangible cultural human historic past. Essentially, French meals is tremendous via the use of its wonderful taste and has endorsed the majority of European culinary traditions.

Furthermore, meals in France is designed to be loved and applied for socializing. Cooking techniques, cuisines, and factors in France, like cultural practices and traditions, range by manner of vicinity. But one factor they all have in commonplace is that the stereotypes about the French and their love of baguettes and cheese are actual!

Fashion in French Society

France has a extended history with fashion and excessive couture. To wholesome in with the natives, it's far going without pronouncing that you want to continually intention to put on your incredible! At the very least, it is able to be remaining to avoid very comfortable garb and appear a touch more "prepare." Wearing corporation informal apparel as often as feasible is a piece of recommendation.

Celebrations and Holidays

The starting of the New Year, Easter Day, Labor Day, Victoria Day, Coronation Day, Pentecost, White Monday, Pastel Day, Virgin's Day, Saints' Day, Warriors' Day, and Christmas are all first rate holidays.

French traditions and behavior: greetings

This is one of the maximum charming French customs: commonly say properly day and goodbye, which consist of welcoming the shopkeeper whenever you enter a employer! Actually, no longer announcing hi there, good-bye, and thanks on the identical time as entering into a small save or café is considered impolite. Formal greetings consist of announcing "bonjour/bonsoir" on every occasion you meet someone, in spite of the truth that they will be strangers. Informal greetings, rather, embody the double take a look at-to-cheek air kiss known as "faire l. A. Bise."

Opening and ultimate instances

Monday morning through Friday night are the legitimate jogging hours for French governmental and private entities. Weekends are Saturday and Sunday, and artwork keeps the subsequent Monday.

Working hours, but, start at 8-thirty within the morning and stop at twelve-thirty in the afternoon. Then an hour and a half for lunch. The undertaking then continues from o'clock inside the afternoon till 5 thirty inside the night time time.

Furthermore, some colleges start 1/2 an hour or an hour past due at maximum. Others extend their artwork hours thru an hour or half of of an hour beyond 5 o'clock. Others, however, finish their interest at four o'clock, and that is determined by way of the use of the inner hints of various groups.

Furthermore, from Monday thru Friday, banks begin their formal business agency through the use of taking clients at nine a.M. And end at five p.M. Furthermore, most banks are open on Saturdays from nine:00 a.M. Till 1:00 p.M. All banks are closed on Sunday.

Post offices perform on the same time desk as banks, irrespective of Saturday's formal business enterprise hours, which might be from eight a.M. To twelve p.M. Every big French city has a located up place of job this is commonly open.

Etiquette for Gift Giving

Gift-giving traditions are a few extraordinary aspect of French etiquette that you want to be aware of to fit in. When touring a person's house for dinner, it is preferred to provide a modest gift for the host. The awesome wager is to ship a touch container of candies, extraordinary candies, or maybe vegetation. Just do no longer carry chrysanthemums at any time, considering they're related to lack of existence in France!

The Significance of Art in French Culture and Heritage

Art has a particular characteristic in French manner of existence, customs, and traditions. French literature, art, and film have made the u . S . Famous for the duration of information, earning France a worldwide popularity in this region. Even now, artwork is held in excessive regard in France. And the internationally diagnosed Louvre, the sector's biggest artwork museum, is a testament to that.

France's Most Renowned and Adored Cuisines and Where To Try Them

French Food in Paris is surely the crucial sort of meals in the metropolis. From high-quality pastries to their conventional cuisine, Paris is the appropriate spot to enjoy some of the city and France's most renowned and loved meals.

It isn't always the excellent chore to locate where to devour some of the ones delicacies in the metropolis considering that Paris has about forty,000 restaurants from which you may pick out. So, we've got made a list of French materials which you ought to strive in Paris and in which to strive them!

If you're a travelling gourmet, you'll without a doubt adore our Eating in Paris professional manual!

Croque Monsieur

This famend sandwich named "Croque Monsieur" become first of all made in 1910 at a modest cafe close to the Paris Opera area. It makes the proper Parisian lunch. It is made from the following components: 2 or three pieces of bread with ham, cheese, butter, and a "bechamel" (a white sauce). The cheese is each in the sandwich and on pinnacle of it. It is roasted until each detail has melted into a particular! And it is then provided to you, normally, with a side salad! You may also have a Croque Madame it is the equal detail however with a fried egg on top.

Where to attempt it: Le Petit Cler Address: 29 Rue Cler, 75007

Le Petit Cler serves an wonderful Croque Monsieur that is high-quality for lunch. Located only a few blocks from the Eiffel Tower, it is a pleasant internet web page online to transport and enjoy a snug lunch after some sightseeing.

Chapter 16: Boeuf Bourguignon

Boeuf Bourguignon is a robust factor of the Burgundy location. However, it's far a French Food this is cherished in Paris and all of France. It is a stewed pork organized in pink wine with onions, mushrooms, and lardons. It is served with potatoes which can be both already in it or provided at the facet. It is a remarkable and rich meal this is simply virtually nicely well worth tasting.

Where to strive it: Chez René

Address: 14 Boulevard Saint-Germain, 75005

Chez Rene is located within the picturesque Saint Germain district. You might also spend some hours right here buying and roaming about after which going to this high-quality French restaurant that is stated for its immoderate superb and scrumptious tasting meals.

Coq au vin

Coq au vin is a braised hen with wine, lardon, and mushrooms. The red wine used to roast the hen regularly originates from Burgundy. However, in plenty of French areas, it is made with loads of wines and it is delicious!

Where to strive it: Buvette Paris Address: 28 Rue Henry Monnier, 75009

Buvette is situated inside the South a part of Pigalle and it is a greater modern shape of French restaurant. Its antique-time café décor and welcoming and attractive food make this restaurant a real treasure! It is an area well nicely well worth trying.

Soupe à l'oignon

Soupe à l'oignon or French Onion soup is a renowned dish in France and all around the globe. Traditionally it's far cooked with pork broth, onions, sherry, and topped with cheese. Better but it's far served with top notch and clean bread. You also can accumulate it as a starting at terrific locations or request it as a meal.

Where to strive it: Le Pied au Cochon

Address: 6 Rue Coquillière, 75001

We recommend trying it at Le Pied The Cochon. Their French Onion Soup is divine and fairly tasty! Their traditional French eating place will make you enjoy like you're again at all over again!

Foie gras

Foie gras originated from the southwestern vicinity of France and it's miles a kind of Pâté organized from duck or goose liver. It is offered as an appetizer before your maximum critical meal. Often it's miles via way of way of agencies slices of bread and a type of jam, typically, fig. It might also moreover sound a piece unstable but we suppose it's miles worth a strive.

Where to strive it: Comptoir de l. A. Gastronomie

Address: 34 Rue Montmartre, 75001

We propose trying it at Comptoir de l. A. Gastronomie. Located inside the stunning

Montmartre community, this restaurant makes a speciality of French meals from the South West. They really have one of the first-rate foie gras within the town so it is a incredible location to attempt it for the primary time!

Escargot

Escargot is a completely unique dish from the Burgundy location in France. While it may seem like a crazy dish to have, it's miles properly worth a try at the same time as you are in Paris. Escargots or snails, in English, are usually cooked of their shell with parsley and butter. You will then get a special fork to take the snail out of its shell to consume it!

Where to try it: L'Escargot

Address: 38 Rue Montorgueil, 75001

No better vicinity to do that than at a place known as L'Escargot. As the decision shows they reputation on escargots! However, don't be fooled; they serve pretty some different French dishes as properly!

Pot au Feu

Pot au Feu is a conventional French dish that dates once more to the 1600s. It is a slow-cooked pork that is cooked with carrots, turnips, leeks, celery, onions, red meat tails, and bones. Typically, consuming locations will serve it with a element bowl of Dijon mustard.

Where to Try It: Le Roi du Pot au Feu

Address: 34 Rue Vignon, 75009

Le Roi du Pot au Feu, because the name suggest, focuses on Pot au Feu. It is the right area to get a outstanding-tasting plate of this conventional French dish! Make fine to pair it with a tumbler of crimson wine.

Steak Frites

Steak and French fries, as it's miles acknowledged in English, is a French dish that may be decided in masses of French bistros. I propose what extra do you need than a fresh piece of steak, fries, and a scrumptious sauce?

Where to strive it: Relais de L'Entrecôte

Address: 20 rue Saint Benoit, 75006

One of the maximum famous steak frites restaurants in Paris is the Relais de L'Entrecôte. Their meat is moderate and scrumptious, their fries are crispy and glowing and their sauce is out of this worldwide. It is the incredible location to attempt it!

Poulet Rôti

"Poulet Rôti" is a roast chook. Plain and simple. But, the sauce it is cooked in is what makes it scrumptious. It is commonly served with roasted or boiled potatoes and vegetables.

Where to Try it: Le Coq Rico

Address: ninety eight Rue Lepic, 75018

You can purchase Poulet Roti at maximum Parisian groceries or markets however in case you need to attempt it at a eating place then we endorse Le Coq Rico. They popularity on chook dishes and their Poulet Roti is amazing!

Creme Brulee

Creme Brulee is one of the most well-known cakes in France. It is a chilly and creamy vanilla custard that is crowned with a skinny, hardened layer of caramelized sugar. It is regularly served in a splendidly sized bowl so that you have just the proper quantity of sweetness after a meal.

www.ingramcontent.com/pod-product-compliance
Lightning Source LLC
Chambersburg PA
CBHW071441080526
44587CB00014B/1942